Voodoo Rituals

Heike Owusu

Sterling Publishing Co., Inc.
New York

Library of Congress Cataloging-in-Publication Data available

10   9   8   7   6   5   4   3

English translation by Inge Lasting

Published by Sterling Publishing Co., Inc.
387 Park Avenue South, New York, N.Y. 10016
Originally published under the title *VooDoo Rituale*
© 2000 by Schirner Verlag, Darmstadt, Germany
English translation © 2002 by Sterling Publishing Co., Inc.
Distributed in Canada by Sterling Publishing
C/o Canadian Manda Group, One Atlantic Avenue, Suite 105
Toronto, Ontario, Canada M6K 3E7
Distributed in Great Britain by Chrysalis Books
64 Brewery Road, London N7 9NT, England
Distributed in Australia by Capricorn Link (Australia) Pty. Ltd.
P.O. Box 704, Windsor, NSW 2756, Australia

Sterling ISBN 1-4027-0035-0

Contents

Contents

Contents

Contents

Contents

Contents

Introduction

The roots of Haitian voodoo lie in Africa. Its conventions later mixed with those of the Indian tribes living in Central and South America. Gods from several other pagan religions were also incorporated in part, but invoked by different names. The term "Voodoo" comes from the language of the African tribes Fon and Eve and means "heavenly intuition, vitality," which expresses the basically positive outlook of the Voodoo religion. Unfortunately, in our cultural environment, Voodoo is still, for the most part, thought of in connection with black magic and satanic practices.

At the core of Voodoo is the recognition that all things, events, and living beings in the entire cosmos are inextricably bound together. This universal spiritual system rests on the common principles of magic.

This book will not be limited to Haitian voodoo. It's not likely that most people would want to take up some of their traditional practices—such as tearing apart a chicken with the teeth or the ritual butchering of a goat. Also, in the Voodoo religion, specific rituals often stretch over several days and are quite expensive. And it would be difficult to organize and attend the ceaseless drumming that sometimes takes place. Great power and influence are ascribed to Haitian Voodoo rituals mainly because they are still practiced so actively and with such intensity. Many people nowadays are not quite sure whether they would be able to withstand the magical attack of a bokor, a Voodoo black magic practitioner. A bokor uses not only spiritual powers, but also a thorough knowledge of toxicology, and would not hesitate to use the most dangerous poisons to harm others. So, in the course of time, an adulteration of Voodoo has taken place, especially in the area of black magic.

I am going to report in this book about the extreme forms of the Voodoo cult for the sake of completeness and in order to point out to possible victims a way to free themselves from these kinds of spells.

The practical use of Voodoo magic is based on two forms. In one of them, small events are created, as in many other magical systems, that are designed to become a reality in the material world. Voodoo doll magic belongs to this realm. In the other form, the gods are invoked directly to assist in magical works. The closest contact with deities in Haitian Voodoo takes place during ceremonies that are conducted on a grand scale, in which it appears that a kind of madness is purposely triggered in the participants. Direct connection with the deities is usually established in this way.

It is especially difficult for those of the Christian religion to understand the Voodoo cult. This has to do mostly with the divine status of all the influential entities in Voodoo and the fact that even the most negative and cruel among them would never be called devils in the Christian sense. Instead, all entities and deities, angels and demons, have their special functions and are honored accordingly. The most dangerous demons may not be liked very much, but they are accorded respect and from time to time presented with offerings to appease them.

Since Voodoo rests on universal magic principles, I will explain them within the framework of the various rituals. This knowledge is indispensable for those who wish to conduct genuine magic and to create a desired reality according to their imagination. For this reason, I have included several exercises that facilitate the strengthening of magical abilities and promote personal growth.

There are some practitioners, of course, who concentrate on the practical use of sorcery in order to create some mischief. They are not released from the responsibility for what they do. Everything that they send out will come back to them tenfold. Caution is always warranted in this practice. Those who employ these techniques are solely responsible for the damage that arises from the misuse of the rituals described here.

The Ambivalence of Magic
(based on a depiction by a Nigerian artist)

Introduction

Basically, everything is permitted in the magical realm that does not cause harm to others. This rule does not apply exclusively to harmful magic. An overwhelming love-magic spell may impede a person's further development and prevent him or her from finding the right partner. In the end, sorcerers only harm themselves with the imprudent use of magic. This is not to say that harmful magic does not have its place—in self-defense, for example. But it is essential to employ a conscientious and appropriate use of these powers.

I have considered the magical practices of many cultures in this book, since they follow the same laws as those of classical Voodoo and they have worked well. I have shortened some rituals that contain Haitian practices that cannot readily be carried out by those of us from different traditions. Their shorter length, however, does not limit their effectiveness. In order to be absolutely sure about this, I established direct contact with some Loa (supernatural beings) who gladly offered their cooperation. Establishing a connection with Haitian Loa is generally simpler than with the deities of other cultures. The reason lies in the fact that they have been uninterruptedly venerated right up to the present time. As a result, they have accrued power and sufficient energy to appear in our material world and intervene in the weaving of reality. They confirm that, as is generally true in magic, it is not important to adhere slavishly to precise instructions for ritual practice, as long as you are careful to obey certain ground rules, especially when invoking spirits. Outside of this precaution, creativity is one of the most important attributes in practical magic.

The magic powers of the practitioners of Haitian Voodoo rest mostly on an oral tradition. This means that a magician or priest passes knowledge on to his students, and they relay it to the next generation. In this way, some important steps that are necessary for the conscientious use of magical powers may be neglected in the training of prospective sorcerers and witches. Most followers of Voodoo are not at all—or not sufficiently—familiar with the larger cosmic nexus. Take ancestor worship, for example. Contrary to popular belief, it is not about the ghosts of deceased people, but about phantoms who have been created artificially through the veneration of a transfigured image of the ancestors. For this reason, I have left out rituals that are connected with ancestor worship. Instead, I have rather thoroughly treated the responsible creation of elementals, which you can direct to carry out your desires, if you wish to avail yourself of this kind of magic.

In compiling this book, I placed great value on information and explanations about cosmic connections, so that here you will not only find the important information that is the basis for successful magic activity, but also knowledge that may be useful to you in your personal spiritual growth.

Black Witchcraft and
Black Magic in Haiti

How seriously black magic is regarded in the countries of the Voodoo cult is evident from the fact that until 1953 it was considered a criminal offense. Even nowadays, officials recognize cases of witchcraft in which human beings have suffered serious harm. Every Haitian knows of at least one such case in his immediate environment and is aware that such happenings occur daily.

Even in our time, many bokors (black magic practitioners) are up to mischief in Haiti. The problem lies in the fact that these sorcerers have not developed their power from their own abilities or from a high developmental stage, but have found a way to connect with the appropriate demons and make contracts with them. There are bokors who will execute all kinds of harmful magic in return for the desired compensation. This irresponsible attitude toward life is often coupled with a brutal sadism.

Even if a misdeed has been carried out by a demon, the sorcerer who gave the order will sooner or later feel its consequences. For one thing, the bokor binds himself to the demon by making a pact with him, and is obligated after his physical death to serve the demon in his world. Many sorcerers are not aware of this fact or they just repress the knowledge of it. For another thing, the bokor is in constant danger that a harmful spell will be recognized and thrown back onto the sender with an immensely increased effect.

Be urgently warned of imitating such practices: everything that you send out will come back to you.

I.

The Loa—Gods of Voodoo

<<< DAM - XX BALAH →→→

Rada- and Petro-Loa

LOA breakdown

Voodoo followers break down the Loa (supernatural beings) into two groups: Rada-Loa and Petro-Loa. The two groups cannot, however, be as strictly separated as, for instance, angels and demons in Christianity. The Loa of the Rada group serve creation, social improvement, and the maintenance of life. These would include deities like the forest god Loco, the ruler of the seas Agwé, and the goddess of beauty Erzulie. They are not very active, so it is not too dangerous to invoke them. Some deities can be assigned to both the Rada and the Petro groups. Legba, for example, the god of the crossroads, can be invoked as a well-meaning Rada-Loa, but also carry out a work of destruction as Petra-Loa. Some people feel that there might be two different Loa at work here, and others say it is the same deity in different aspects.

The pure Petro-Loa are a group of demons who are invoked primarily for harmful sorcery. The core in such a ritual is the Petro-Loa symbol (see the illustration on page 17) used in connection with the vèvè of the deity being invoked.

It is interesting that many of these Loa do not stem from the African tradition, but were adopted from the mythology of the native tribes who originally inhabited Haiti and the other islands. It is this mixture of two mighty cults that makes Haitian Voodoo so dangerous. To invoke a Petra-Loa can involve great dangers for body and soul, and especially those who are unprepared are urgently advised to refrain from using it.

Some of the original demons are even these days used by native sorcerers in Venezuela and Colombia. Brutality and cruelty are commonplace for the Petro-Loa. Therefore, to invoke them, it is essential to make a blood sacrifice, usually in the form of a black goat or a black chicken. The animal, by the way, must consent to its sacrifice. To get the animal to consent, it is given food. If it accepts it, this is taken as agreement. If it refuses, it is led away and replaced by another animal.

Furthermore, possession by a Petro-Loa can carry with it great dangers for the possessed person. With some members of the Petro-Loa group, possession must absolutely be prevented, since the Loa would immediately kill their human "horse" as a welcome sacrificial offering. Despite their bloodthirsty inclinations, the Petro-Loa are not regarded as demonic beings by followers of Voodoo. They are respected in their field. After all, with appropriate compensation, they can also be enlisted for protection from black magic.

Legba or Elegba, Eshu, Ellegua

Attributes: God of the crossroads, singer, warrior, jester, guardian of the door to the world of spirits. He often appears as a child or a crippled old man.

Sacred places: The crossroads of the world

Day: Monday

Colors: Black, red

Number: Three

Favorite food: Sweets, maize, and rum

Planet: Mercury

Ritual place in the house: Behind the door

Salutation: Ago Ellegua

The worship of Legba has its origin in Dahomey, present-day Benin. There, Legba was seen as a radiantly beautiful, young god and, therefore, he was often pictured with the cosmic phallus, a symbol of his life-conferring attributes (see the illustration on page 18).

In the Haitian Voodoo cult, Legba is worshiped in both his contrasting incarnations: the child, and the crippled old man, walking with a cane. In both incarnations, Legba is quick and unpredictable. He is regarded as a trickster and as a personal messenger of fate. As a child, he is rebellious; as an old man, wise. In some myths, he is also portrayed as a thief, because he is said to have stolen some divine secrets and revealed them to human beings.

According to legend, he is the youngest son of Lisa and Mawu. Lisa is the sun god who brings the day and the heat, and also strength and energy. Mawu, the moon goddess, provides the cool of the night, peace, fertility, and rain. Thus, Legba combines all these attributes, and in his role as god of fate, he can bring great fortune but also unspeakable sorrow to man.

Every ceremony begins with his invocation and ends with his dismissal. It is only through contact with Legba that it becomes possible to contact the other gods, for he is the guardian at the door of the world of spirits. During an invocation, he mostly appears as the messenger of another god, translating the words of the supernatural into the language of humans.

The holy center of each Voodoo temple is a column decorated with consecrated signs. It embodies the cosmic channel through which communication with the world of the spirits becomes possible. Legba is the guardian of this bridge between worlds, which also connects the place of the living with the realm of the dead. Therefore, with Legba's consent it is possible for the dead to return to the world of the living. Ghosts of these ancestors return either to protect their families, or to take revenge if they have been neglected.

Legba's vèvè (shown on the next page) is sketched on the ground at the beginning of every ceremony. In Haiti, it includes the

symbol of a crutch. His invocation is
sung by the participants in unison:

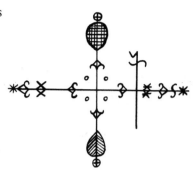

Atibon Legba, open the gate for me.
Papa Legba, open the gate for me.
Open the gate that I can enter.
God Legba, open the gate for me.
When I return, I will thank the Loa.
Abobo!

Meanwhile, the Voodoo priest runs again and again to the door to symbolically open it, until finally Legba takes possession of one of the people present. Then it is said that the Loa "rides" him. The person possessed by Legba takes on the appearance of an old man, immediately beginning to limp—and his limbs are often forcibly twisted in such a way that he is indeed temporarily crippled. In this manner, Legba demonstrates the terrible strength he possesses, despite his appearance as a weak, old man.

After Legba has manifested himself in this way, the other gods can be called.

Legba's altar is on the ground, in a box, or a closet behind the entrance to the house. He is supplied with food items that are associated with him, and also with fabrics and pearls in his black and red colors.

When a person turns to him, Legba is first greeted with the ritual "Ago Ellegua!" He is mostly called upon when the person seeking help has to make a decision and can no longer clearly see his course. The god can then lead him and open the way for him.

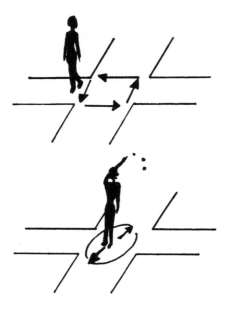

Road Magic

You need three shining coins and a lonely crossroads, in a forest, for instance. Hold the coins in your right hand while telling them your desire. Then, take them into your left hand and tell them which paths you could take to reach your destination. Now, hold both hands together and squeeze the coins between them. Ask Legba for his guidance, and then walk once around the inner square that is formed by the corners of the roads. Stop for a moment on every corner. Then walk once diagonally over the crossing and, after arriving in the center, throw the coins over your left shoulder. Avoid turning around when leaving the location; turn your thoughts toward other things—let the deity regulate your actions. Legba is able to influence people and situations, so suitable circumstances will soon come about for you, and your path will be clearly recognizable.

Coconut Child

This is protective sorcery conducted by the head of a witch circle for her pupil. As a precondition, both women must have a good, loving relationship, and the woman who works the magic must be the more powerful one.

The pupil selects from her favorite marketplace a coconut that in some way reminds her of her teacher. This is the coconut-child. It is important that there is still milk inside it. The coconut-child is placed behind the door of the pupil's house for three days. The pupil goes on to ask Legba for his blessings. After three weeks, the pupil gives the coconut to her spiritual guide, who washes it in spring water, sprinkles it with earth from a sacred place, and covers it with incense. Next, she holds it over a white candle until the incense and the small hairs have been burned way. Meanwhile, she gives the coconut-child the good wishes and requests of the pupil. This supplication is repeated several times on three consecutive days in front of a white candle and a glass of water. After that, the coconut-child is set on the altar, where it lies for three days. After this time, it is painted.

Road crossings are a favorite subject to draw on the coconut and they are painted in white (see below). The fields that are created can be filled with symbols and colors that lend strength and power.

When this part of the ceremony is complete, the sorceress ties together the long hairs at the end of the coconut and fastens three little bells to them. Then she puts the coconut behind her own house door for another three days, and thanks Legba for protecting her pupil's house. Now the coconut-child is ready and is handed back to the pupil who will either hang it on her house door or place it behind the door. It is customary for her to thank her spiritual guide by giving her a gift or money.

Shango or Xango, Chango

Attributes: God of the fire, warrior, judge, ruler over lightning and thunder—courageous, hot-tempered, and handsome

Sacred places: Heaven, trees, Trinidad

Symbols: Double ax, forest, horse, ram, pigeon, pheasant

Day: Friday

Colors: Red, white

Number: Six

Favorite food: Maize, pepperoni, apple, yam roots

Planets: Mars, Sun

Ritual place in the house: Fireplace, desk

Salutation: Kaguo Kabiosile

Originally, Shango was revered by the Yoruba, a tribe in what is present-day Nigeria. Although he is one of the mightiest of the seven major Loa, he is not invoked as often as the others these days in Haiti. He was born as one of the earth gods and at first lived together with humans, where he reigned in the kingdom of Oyo. All during his earthly life, he prepared for his divine existence, and various magic powers were already ascribed to him during his lifetime. Often,

23

flames came out of his mouth, and he could hurl lightning bolts on his enemies—an ability that his priests were also said to possess. In earlier times, people killed by lightning bolts were simply carried into the woods and forgotten. It was assumed that they were evil-doers—thieves, black magicians, and other criminals—whom Shango always punished severely, and therefore just punishment had been meted out to them.

When once his subjects voiced their dissatisfaction with him, he ascended to heaven on a golden chain. Nowadays, he is worshiped as god of justice and often depicted together with his three wives, Oba, Oya, and Oshun. Shango's power is embodied on the altar of a house by a double-bladed ax or a ram's antlers. The double-bladed ax signifies life as a two-sided thing.

An invocation of Shango can assist in court proceedings and lend courage and energy. During ceremonies, he displays an invulnerability toward fire. This link to fire makes him helpful with illnesses that can be cured by means of the fire-element.

Justice Magic

Six red apples are needed for this ritual. They must be well-cooled in the refrigerator to facilitate the absorption of energy. Line a wooden bowl, which has been purified by the sorceress, with cotton balls. Then fetch the apples. The sorceress rubs down her whole body with them, while telling Shango of all the injustices she has suffered. Then, she places the apples in the bowl, together with six whole red chilis, and pours honey over them until the fruits are covered. When she has finished, she takes the bowl into the forest, puts it under a tree, and yields the offering to Shango to complete the desired solution to the affair.

Oshun or Oxum, Ezili, Erzulie

Attributes: Goddess of love and of creative powers, mistress of abundance and passion—beautiful, seductive, young
Sacred places: Mountains, running waters, Oshun/Nigeria, Cuba
Symbols: Jewelry, mirror, fans, gold, little bells, parrot, peacock, quail, clams, hawk
Day: Thursday
Colors: Coral-red, yellow, green
Number: Five
Favorite food: Cake, oranges, cinnamon, honey, melon
Planets: Venus, waxing Moon
Ritual place in the house: Bedroom, kitchen
Salutation: Ori Ye Ye O

Oshun is the African Venus or Aphrodite. She stands for beauty, sensuality, and love. In Nigeria she has been revered for a long time as the goddess of the river Oshun. A festival in her honor is celebrated every year, where food is abundant and distributed liberally. During the dances that take place, the goddess selects suitable women as intermediaries. They will stay in contact with the goddess for the rest of their lives and receive the surname Oshun. The advice of these women is sought, usually about questions of health and matters of love.

In Haiti, Oshun is worshiped as Erzulie, the divine concubine. None of her liaisons last very long. She was married for a short time to Shango, the god of fire, but since then has had numerous affairs with other gods and men.

Erzulie resides over the fine arts, such as painting and sculpture, and all jewels belong to her. Her task is to spread the love of life and passion.

She heals the sick over the cool waters that also belong within

EZILI FRÉDA

her realm. Her generosity nourishes the hungry. She spreads cosmic abundance so that all can enjoy the beauty of creation.

Yet we need to be careful. Erzulie is also the mother of the witches and paints herself with her enemies' blood. Hawks, too, are under her power. By using her feminine lures, the goddess understands intuitively how to get everything she wants from men and male gods. And Erzulie knows what she wants.

In every temple in Haiti, a small room or an altar is devoted to the goddess. She is typically a sorceress-goddess, consulted mostly by women. When Erzulie reveals herself after the ceremony invoking the Loa, she appears as a charming, young mulatto with loosened hair, draped in a rose-colored or yellow gown. When she has taken possession of an individual, the possessed person, usually a female, is led to her altar on which various toiletries are kept so that she can groom herself. There is a bowl of water for washing up, a towel, a comb, a toothbrush, a nail file, lipstick, and other make-up items. She seldom chooses to possess a man, but she does so on and off, when the fancy strikes her, and also to contribute to the general amusement: The possessed individual immediately begins to sway the hips and starts flirting with the men present. Erzulie also likes to kiss and caress the participants. She greatly welcomes presents, which she does not keep but lavishly distributes. She often treats women disdainfully, greeting them only by extending her little finger.

Erzulie has nothing in common with the motherly fertility goddess—she embodies free love, flirtation, and a luxurious lifestyle. She is also the patroness of followers of Voodoo and prostitutes. The heart on her vèvè, pierced by a lance (page 26), portrays the many broken hearts of the men she leaves behind on her path. As a mulatto with dark skin, she also mirrors the racial bias in Haiti. She will not submit to the black-skinned dead persons' Loa Guédé-Nibo. Although he has long been pining for her, she rejects his love.

Ritual for Prosperity, Beauty, Love, and Health

Make a string of pearls with little bells on it, and buy a feathered fan that you spray with an expensive perfume. Place a bowl with honey on your altar and put into it five each of vanilla sticks, pumpkin pits, cloves, dashes of nutmeg, and cinnamon sticks. Stand in front of the altar, arms stretched out, and beg Oshun to fulfill your wishes. Make your entreaty in clear and unambiguous words. In addition, remind the goddess to send her riches to the whole world so that all people will have enough food, health, and love.

Oya or Yansa, Aida-Wedo, Olla

Attributes: Goddess of the wind, fire, water, rainbow; ruler over the forces of nature; warrior—courageous, beautiful, passionate, and unpredictable

Sacred Places: Wind, the rivers Amazon and Niger

Symbols: Copper, black horse hair, sheep, locusts, electrical switches

Day: Wednesday

Colors: Purple, brown, red, terra-cotta (burned earth)

Number: Nine

Favorite food: Eggplant, blue grapes, plums, red wine

Planets: Uranus, new moon

Ritual place in the house: Office, book corner

Salutation: Hekua Oya

Oya is the goddess of sudden changes. This energy is expressed in the strength of her destructive powers, which can bring about tornadoes, torrential rains, and earthquakes. One moment she acts meek as a lamb, swinging a rainbow over the landscape, and in the moment that follows she can destroy whole regions with a tremendous storm. Her constant aim is to bring about change and to break apart old structures. Her frenzied dancing keeps the world moving. She influences the human spirit, conferring intuition and talents as well as feeble mindedness. Oya's power lies in her swiftness and ability to transform. The West-African river Niger is considered an outward manifestation of the goddess.

29

If Oya appears in a Voodoo ceremony, the possessed individual dances wildly and frantically, in most cases, holding a torch in the right hand and making movements with it that suggest the setting afire of nearby buildings or trees.

Ritual for Change

An altar of Oya should have on it all the things that are associated with the goddess. When the time is ripe for undertaking important changes, carry out the following ritual. But take care to state your request precisely and be prepared for really consequential, sudden, and unexpected changes.

Select a well-rounded eggplant and wash it with red wine. Now, take a wide, dark orange ribbon and fasten to it nine ribbons in

different colors. Hold the eggplant, "clothed" in this "skirt," in your right hand, and keep turning it counter-clockwise, while you state the plans with which you want Oya to assist.

In order to give more impetus to the magic, place a silver bolt, made out of cardboard and silver paper, on the goddess's altar. Also very useful is a broom, with ribbons in Oya's colors attached, for sweeping old and past events out of the house.

Put the eggplant on your altar. If it withers, take it to the forest and leave it there. If you have no altar, take it directly to the forest.

Yemaya or Imanje, La Balianne

Attributes: Female goddess of the oceans—motherly, nourishing, loving, and desirable

Sacred Places: Ocean coast, Brazil, the river Ogun/Nigeria

Symbols: Shells, rattles, glittering clothes, crystal pearls, bird (sandpiper), cockroaches

Day: Saturday

Colors: White, blue, silver

Number: Seven

Favorite food: Watermelon, molasses, maize flour

Planets: Neptune, full moon

Ritual place in the house: Bathroom, bedroom, nursery

Salutation: Omio Yemaya

Yemaya rules over the oceans and is the embodiment of female power. She guards all the nourishing entities and orders women's affairs. Her figure is large and dark, her body that of a seductive mermaid. In Africa, among the Yoruban peoples of Nigeria, she is worshiped as the mother of the river Ogun. A pitcher with water from the Ogun is believed to be a remedy for infertile women. As thanks, the goddess receives sacrifices such as poultry, fish, roots of yams, and cowrie shells, which represent riches.

Yemaya protects the fetus in the womb and guards the household. Like the waters over which she rules, the goddess is crystal-clear and shining at the same time that she is mysteriously dark and unfathomably deep. She has nurturing as well as consuming powers. Her task is steady renewal. In many countries, festivals in her honor are held during the nights of the full moon.

A goddess who manifests in two different ways, she appears as La Balianne and the Siren at Voodoo ceremonies in Haiti. Both forms are invoked with the same song and worshiped in the same

31

manner. Individuals possessed by the goddess conduct themselves in a markedly elegant and superior manner; sometimes she is also youthfully coquettish. Noticeable is her flawless French.

Yemaya's Letterbox

Yemaya's altar should be abundantly and beautifully decorated. It is important to have on it all the items that are associated with the goddess. In order to enhance her presence, add a flat bowl or a jar with a blue-white cover that has been filled with sea water or water from a well plus sea salt. Place in it shells, pearls, crystals, silver jewelry, and a small figurine of a mermaid. Then charge the bowl with the energy of the goddess in the light of the full moon, and thereafter it will serve as a means of communication. Through this bowl, all important concerns can be communicated to Yemaya.

Petition Magic

This magic is recommended for desires concerning matters of love, new lodgings, or the wish for a child.

Begin by making a hole in a watermelon (or a pineapple) that is big enough to hold a candle. Then, pour molasses over the fruit, trickle maize powder on it, and finally insert a dark blue candle deeply into the hole. At sunrise, take the fruit to a body of water—a

lake, a river, or the ocean—put it down at the edge and make a circle around it with the seven coins. They represent the full moon. Light the candle and tell Yemaya your wishes while facing the water.

You can thus wash away troubles and sorrow with the waters of the goddess. Yet it can be dangerous to bathe in them while you are telling her about your grief. You could experience what has already happened to many women—that the goddess out of empathy takes you along or swallows you up. It is safer to establish the connection to Yemaya from the shore and to look into her shimmering face from a distance.

be mindful
of
her abundance

Obatala or Oxala, Batala, Blanc, Dani

Attributes: Hermaphrodite god, embodying the energy of creation—
old and white-haired, kind, immensely powerful

Sacred places: Clouds, the city Ife-Ife/Nigeria

Symbols: Coconuts, grapes, elephants, snails, owls, white garments,
cotton balls

Day: Sunday

Colors: White with silver, and also purple

Number: Eight

Favorite food: Coconut, peas, pears, cola nuts (chewing the seeds
causes a condition similar to intoxication)

Planet: Jupiter

Ritual place in the house: A raised place in the living room

Salutation: Maferefun Ba Ba

Obatala is the creative god of the Yorubans (peoples who live in the
area now known as Nigeria). His/her name signifies the concept of
God as such. Male and female at the same time, Obatala is portrayed
as an old man (Baba-father) or an old woman (Iya-mother) with
white hair. He is looked upon as the direct descendant of the
highest, omnipresent god Olodumare. He divided the world into the
various areas of life, assigned animals and men to their niches, and
transformed the land into a fertile garden. The Yorubans also called
Obatala the sculptor god who artfully creates every live, growing
thing. He likes order and cleanliness, drapes himself in shining white
robes and lives in a meticulously snow-white palace. A pitcher of
fresh, clean water is always in his sanctum for medicinal purposes.
A maiden or an old woman renews the water every morning.

Ruler of the brain and the spiritual powers, Obatala embodies
the high ethical virtues of justice, wisdom, intelligence, and magna-
nimity, observing human development from the clouds and from the

peaks of the highest mountains. He teaches humility to the haughty, brings abundance and variety, and heals fatal illnesses. Constantly at work to maintain his creation, Obatala is an ally in the fight for the environment.

Obatala's altar in the home should be on a raised stand or platform. In addition to the items assigned, you might add a figurine that expresses compassion, and hang up a "peace cloud" in the room (see the illustration at the right).

⚡Extrication from Dependencies Ritual ⚡

This ritual serves to eradicate undesirable habits and dependencies, such as on drugs or alcohol, that contaminate body and soul.

Peel eight potatoes, boil them, and mash them. To the mashed potatoes add a teaspoon of vegetable extract and a package of ground coconut. From this mixture form eight little balls—all of the same size—and pile them up in a bowl that is clad in white lace. At this point, you address the pile of potato balls with your problems and desires. You need to exhale on it with cool breath after every sentence. Then, on a Sunday, carry the bowl to a mountain or to a park, preferably on top of your head. There, remove the potato balls from the bowl by wrapping them tightly in the lace cloth, and place the offering under a bush. You can take the bowl home with you and use it later for other purposes.

Ogun or Ogum, Ogu

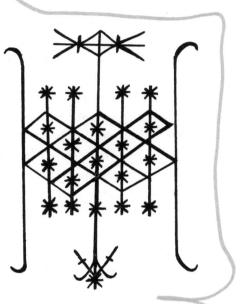

Attributes: The wild man of the
woods, god of iron and
wrought-iron work, protector
of wealth and work—quiet,
dangerous

Sacred places: Deep forests, also
America (god of pioneers)

Symbols: Machete, ax, iron, dog,
goat, rooster

Day: Tuesday

Colors: Green, black—also red, as
a god of war

Numbers: Three and four

Favorite food: Meat, roots, nuts,
and berries

Planets: Pluto and Saturn

Ritual place in the house: Behind the front door or in the garden

Salutation: Onile Ogun

The Nigerian god Ogun long ago made the wild forests on the
newly-created earth traversable for the gods. He created the
machete and the ax and cleared the roads with them. Therefore, he
is called the god of the pioneers, and "The one who opens the way."
Ogun taught men to make brush knives for defending themselves,
to forge iron, and to build houses for their protection. That makes
him the father of civilization and technology. According to legend,
the people once wanted to crown him king, but after he had taught
men everything, he returned the crown and went back into the
forest.

Ogun is strong and stocky, and he covers his hairy body with

37

animal hides. He is a silent, untiring worker who has no inclination for comfort or luxury. Taxi- and truck drivers, tradesmen, mechanics, and soldiers even today ask him for assistance.

In present times in Haiti, Ogun is seen primarily in his capacity as Warrior-Loa. His altar is marked by a saber, which is stuck into the ground in front of him. He loves fire. When individuals are possessed by him, they act as though they are handling glowing iron bars or washing their hands in burning rum. He is not presented with an offering of a drink when he is invoked, since he avoids all water in keeping with his fiery nature. When he has taken possession of an individual, he often makes himself known by calling out "Blast!!" and immediately asking for the white rum, which he drinks in great quantity and pours on the ground in order to light it. Ogun never gets drunk, despite his profuse alcohol consumption. He always retains his upright posture and is the embodiment of strength and manly energy. Those possessed by him are endowed with an enveloping invincibility so strong that even the blade of a saber cannot hurt them.

During Haitian voodoo ceremonies, Ogun appears in various forms, all of which have corresponding names. Common to all of them, however, is his typical conduct and clothing: Ogun is dressed like a soldier at the time of the Haitian Civil War (about 1800) with a French military cap and a red dolman (a laced jacket). As a substitute, red fabric is often draped around his arms and forehead. He chews carelessly on a cigar and conducts himself like a true swordsman and lady-killer. A weakness for beautiful women can drive him to the edge of ruin. He may forgo his meal so that he can pamper the one he adores. He has a passionate relationship with the love goddess Erzulie, who is married to the (subordinate) sea god Agwé—another reason for him to avoid water!

A tripod kettle (see the illustration on the next page) belongs on Ogun's altar to enforce his power. This, by the way, is also a symbol in European witchcraft. The kettle must never be cleaned with

water; instead the dirt is removed with a metal brush. The kettle is regularly treated with vegetable oil and filled with iron screws, nails, and tools of all kinds. These contents should also be oiled once in a while.

Advancement Magic

The following magic is used to obtain protection or to end a war. If you like to work, you can also use it to get a well-paying job.

Obtain the "Seven-African-Powers Ingredients"—a ready-to-use product, or you can manufacture it yourself by painting a picture of the seven major African gods or by placing a typical symbol of each of them in a satchel. The seven major African powers are: Legba, Shango, Oshun, Oya, Yemaya, Obatala, and Ogun. Buy or form a seven-powers candle—it is important that it has all the colors of the seven gods.

Now, in a letter to Ogun, describe your concern in explicit, clear words and ask him for help. Place the candle on top of the letter and burn it over nine days' time. During this period, carry the satchel with the seven-powers charm on your body. In addition, you can burn incense during the ritual.

If you are looking for work, visit places where you might find work during each of those nine days, or apply to firms for which you would like to work. Also explore ideas for self-employment.

If you would like to end a war or ask for protection, present your request to Ogun every day as long as the candle is burning.

After the end of nine days, wrap all these magical items in a cloth of the god's color, and add nuts, berries, and leaves. Place the package under a tree in the forest as an offering.

Agwé or Agwé-Taroyo

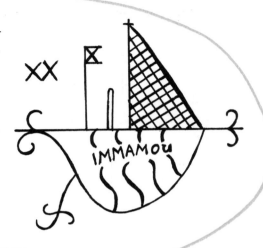

Attributes: God of the waters, master of the seas—beautiful, proud, orderly, well-groomed

Sacred places: Oceans, lakes, rivers

Symbols: Shells, starfish, ships, fish, sponges, the trident, tadpoles

Favorite food: Champagne, seafood, white chicken, white sheep

Color: White

The god of the oceans embodies primarily the useful forms of water. Of all the Loa, he is the most stable character and his tasks are clearly outlined: He is responsible for the animal world and the plants in all the waters of the earth, maintaining their natural order. He is often compared to Poseidon, the Greek god of the sea, from whom the trident symbol was probably adopted. At Haitian ceremonies, Agwé always appears in the uniform of a marine officer, with helmet and gloves. He likes military discipline and conducts himself remarkably well. He is rather reserved and quiet, a god who often appears only indirectly through his unfaithful wife Erzulie (see page 25), who keeps the followers of Voodoo breathless with her numerous affairs. This wins him the sympathy of these onlookers.

Voodoo ceremonies honoring Agwé are held on the beach or on the banks of a lake. After his vèvè, which always pictures him as a sailing ship (he is sometimes also portrayed as a fish) has been drawn, there is drumming and dancing and sometimes salutes are fired (the god is especially fond of that). Then, a small ship or a raft, decorated with symbols of the sea, is loaded with offerings. His followers climb on board and drive a ways out in the water. There, the sacrificial offerings are thrown overboard and champagne, which the god loves especially, is poured into the water. During the return voyage, his followers must be careful that possessed individuals do not fall into the water and that none of them look back, which would insult the god. After the return to shore, the festival honoring Agwé continues. If he does not want to accept the offerings, he washes them back onto the beach—a sure sign to his petitioners that they have to appease the god with another ceremony.

Agwé is called upon to calm the waters or for a safe voyage. He is invoked also by fishermen and those whose livelihoods depend on the preservation of the waters. Those who are under his protection will not be drowned or harmed by water. It has been reported that people who were shipwrecked or stranded, but spiritually connected with the god, reached faraway shores without tiring, not even noticing the great distance and the danger they were in.

Damballah or Aida-Wedo

Attributes: Early original god,
   serpent god (in the shape
   of a snake), cosmic archetypal power, guardian of
   the trees and waters—
   temperamental, severe, and
   courageous
Sacred places: Peaks of trees,
   waters
Symbols: Snake, water basin,
   thunderbolt, the metal
   silver
Favorite food: Milk, milk rice,
   flour, sugar water, eggs—all foods and drinks that are white in
   color
Colors: White, silver

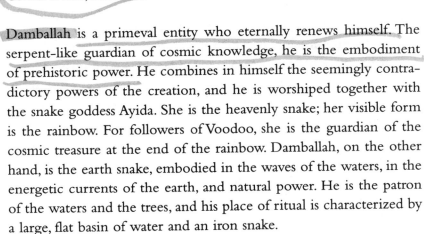

‹‹‹ DAM - ✳✳ BALAH →››

Damballah is a primeval entity who eternally renews himself. The serpent-like guardian of cosmic knowledge, he is the embodiment of prehistoric power. He combines in himself the seemingly contradictory powers of the creation, and he is worshiped together with the snake goddess Ayida. She is the heavenly snake; her visible form is the rainbow. For followers of Voodoo, she is the guardian of the cosmic treasure at the end of the rainbow. Damballah, on the other hand, is the earth snake, embodied in the waves of the waters, in the energetic currents of the earth, and natural power. He is the patron of the waters and the trees, and his place of ritual is characterized by a large, flat basin of water and an iron snake.

In Haiti, as opposed to many other cultures, snakes are not considered direct manifestations of God and are not kept in Voodoo temples. The killing of a snake, therefore, is not a reprehensible act. If snakes are worshiped directly, they are thought of only as intermediaries delivering messages and petitions to God.

Followers of Voodoo are generally very interested in connecting with the primeval power of the Snake God, even though he has very little influence upon their daily lives. Damballah and Ayida are considered to be personalities who are far removed from the world, invoked primarily when people want to be charged with vital energy. There are, however, some select ones toward whom Damballah is especially well disposed and to whom he gives special protection. It sometimes happens that the god unites in a spiritual marriage with a woman possessed by him. Such a marriage takes place like any marriage ceremony on earth, with witnesses and before a Voodoo priest. The agreement calls for the god to protect his wife as long as she lives and supply her with all material goods. In return, he can occupy her body at any time.

Individuals possessed by Damballah move in a snakelike manner. They leap up and hiss, writhe around on the ground, creep up trees and into the joists of a house, where they often hang upside down like boas. Sometimes they even let themselves fall head first, without harming themselves. Since some want to throw themselves into the water, a flat tub or basin, in which they cannot easily drown, is available at the place of rituals. Damballah often puts his human "horse," as the possessed ones are called, in jeopardy by leaving his host when he is up in the peak of a tree from which it is hard to come down. Other participants make a sacrificial offering and engage in great efforts to induce the god to leave a tree or other dangerous place as quickly as possible.

It is often difficult to understand the god's messages because he communicates with hissing and whistling sounds. In most cases, the god Ogun (see page 37) helps out as translator. If he is not present, one of the chief priests can assume the task.

The Snake Movement

Snakelike movements can bring about a condition of trance, because they stimulate the chakras, the energy centers of our body-soul, and can awaken the Kundalini, the snake power. Thus, snake movement is perfectly suited for the preparation of the various invocation rituals.

To perform the snake movement, stand as straight and erect as possible, with your feet parallel to each other. Then form a hollow back and bend your upper body down to your legs while exhaling. Now, push your hips forward, arch your back, and slowly assume an erect posture again by moving from vertebra to vertebra of the spinal column and inhaling. Bend forward again while also lightly bending your knees. When you stand up again, also lift your right leg. When you bend down again, place your weight on only the ball of your foot. Now get up again, do your next step with your left leg, and proceed by alternating the movements. As you do this exercise, try to imitate the movements of a snake, and walk only on the balls of your feet. Always inhale when assuming the erect position and exhale while bending forward, voicing a forceful "O."

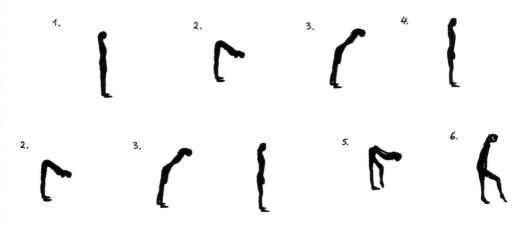

Damballah Magic

A petition to Damballah should have as little as possible to do with matters of daily life. However, the god may be asked for power, strength, wealth, a cure, or cosmic knowledge. To this purpose, go near a spring or a brook. There, speak your wish onto a ribbon and fasten it to the branches of a large tree. In addition, leave at the water's edge a small offering of Damballah's favorite food on a piece of white cloth.

Loco

Another primeval god is the god Loco. He is the invisible spirit of vegetation, a human-like form of plant. Legend has it that Loco was the first priest who changed from man to Loa. Therefore, he is a mediator between man and the gods. Voodoo, like most nature religions, views trees as direct channels or links between the worlds. Loco is the patron of all healers who work with the powers of plants. Before a treatment is started, the god is invoked and begged for support, for only through his power may the seekers receive the healing of the leaves and herbs near the trees. Sacrificial offerings in his name are tied to the branches of tall trees. In Haiti, small satchels with presents are usually hung onto the branches of the wool- or cheese tree, which is especially sacred to the god. If Loco appears at a ceremony, he can be recognized by the knotty stick he carries, or by the pipe-smoking servant who always accompanies him.

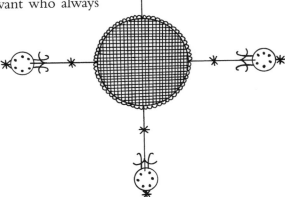

✳꜀꜀꜀ LOCO ꜀꜀꜀✳

Zaka or Azacca

Zaka is another god of the plants whose range of action is the cultivated land. The individual possessed by him wears a blue shirt and straw hat, according to the farmers' customs. This god prefers plain food, such as bread dipped in olive oil, corn meal, and fat meat. He also likes liquor and white rum. Zaka is especially fond of country people and likes to attend to their concerns, if the required sacrificial offerings are made to him in the fields. He is distrustful of city folk. In terms of character, he has much in common with the farmers of 19th-century Middle America. He likes to trade, is very anxious to make a profit, disdains luxury, and lives in the steady fear of being robbed.

Simbi

The Simbi are godly entities of the waters; they are the watchmen of wells and swamps. In appearance, they can hardly be distinguished from the snake god Damballah (see page 43), and their symbol is also a snake. The vèvè pictured here includes a water basin—as does Damballah's—and also several burial-place crosses indicating the Simbi's closeness to the spirits of the dead.

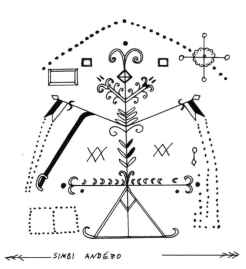

— SIMBI ANDÉZO —

Far more, however, than Damballah, the Simbi are dependent on the element of water: If a participant in a ceremony is possessed by a Simbi, he painfully writhes on the ground and gasps for breath until he is put into the tub or water basin.

Children, especially those who are light-skinned, are quite often kidnapped while going to a well to fetch water. The water spirits pull them down into their realm and make them their servants. Years later, when they are released again, they receive as thanks the gift of fortune-telling and clairvoyance.

The Simbi embody the principle of water, the unknown spiritual depths, the unconscious. They occupy a kind of intermediary position between men and the supernatural, since Voodoo followers envision the mythical "other world" as being deep in the sea. You can call on them to obtain protection with all kinds of magical works.

49

The Gédé or Guédé

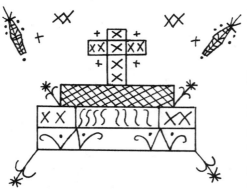

The Gédé have to do with death and the dead. A larger Voodoo ceremony generally ends with the appearance of these death demons, even when they have not been invited. The members of the Gédé family (the sketch on the left shows their vèvè) are only called if a connection to ancestral spirits has been established. They do not have followers as such and lead a rather lonesome existence, eagerly pursuing human life on earth and ridiculing it shamelessly when it appears. They have soaked up in themselves the knowledge of the dead over many generations. This makes them extremely wise advisors who like to reveal themselves if they are asked for help.

Baron Samedi is the head of the family. He appears in three different forms: as Baron Cimetière (in French, this means "cemetery"), as Baron La-Croix (this means Baron of the Cross—his symbol is at the right), and as Baron Samedi (this means Saturday). His distinguishing marks are a cane and a black cross with equally long crossbeams, and he appears in a black suit and hat, standing on a fake gravestone (see sketch on page 51).

Some members of the Gédé

family like to carry picks or shovels. Their clothes are in keeping with their environment, but at the same time seem frightening and a bit ridiculous. They are clothes of mourning of all kinds, usually an old, torn dress coat or tailcoat, and the hat is an old-fashioned derby or a cylinder; sometimes also there is a violet veil.

It is their aim to dress like undertakers and mourners. They have a marked preference for black-tinted sunglasses, which they often steal from onlookers who wear them, two or three pairs at a time.

Other Gédé force possessed individuals to masquerade as corpses—publicly appearing like this during the daytime, especially on All Souls' Day. Although they often frighten the people at first, they arouse general amusement by their wit and suggestiveness, which makes them welcome guests at every festivity.

Typical for members of this family are a nasal twang and risqué expressions that may embarrass even sophisticated people. Phallic symbols are also among their distinguishing features, reminding everyone of the cycle of life. For a follower of Voodoo, death means rebirth on another level. It is significant that the Gédé prefer to take possession of those who conduct themselves with particular chastity and morality in daily life and make them do the "banda," a kind of comically exaggerated mating dance. The Gédé again and again refer—with erotic and provocative gestures—to the creation of new life out of death.

Since they take great liberties for themselves and sexual license, those who seem to be possessed by them are thoroughly tested in order to make sure they are not pretending. An individual who is possessed by the Gédé holds his breath in and throws himself to the ground. When he stands up again, a brew from sugar cane liquor with 21 caustic, pungent herbs is given to him by the priest or poured into his eyes! Only a body that is indeed possessed by a Gédé can endure this procedure unharmed. The brew, by the way, is the Gédé family's favorite drink.

The possessed ones constantly smoke cigarettes and cigars, and drink spirits (rum, especially)—even pouring it into their ears. They greedily gulp down the food offered and bury leftovers in the ground in order to partake of them days later. In this way they satirically mirror the human hunger for life. At the end, the Gédé like to present—in their nasal voices—the undertaker's song that they finish with roaring laughter.

The best-known female Gédé and mother of most of the family members is Madame Brigitte. Her bony figure is generally considered repulsive. A peculiarity is the child-Loa Linto, who also belongs to the Gédé family. The individual possessed by him behaves like an infant who has just learned to walk. He is also treated like a child by the other participants in the ceremony and is sometimes fed baby food.

Evil Loa

In addition to the Gédé, there are some very dangerous entities who are not well inclined toward humans either. The Loa Criminél belongs to them. Immediately after he appears, he tries to eat the individual possessed by him. This can lead to serious mutilations, when the possessed bites into his own flesh. Similar consequences occur when a person is possessed by Jean-Zandor, who is considered violent and irascible. A short man, hopping on one leg, he hunts men in order to consume them. Or, he may throw himself from the peak of a palm tree onto unsuspecting passers-by. If such a possession occurs during a ceremony, the priests and other participants will try to end it immediately, before the possessed suffers harm. They may, for instance, explode gun powder next to the affected person, in order to distract the Loa, or even chase him off.

Another dangerous Loa is the devilish Krabinay, a really evil character. He mostly moves in large jumps and often attacks onlookers. Nevertheless, he supports priests and magicians at work and offers help and healing in the most powerful black magic procedures. Therefore, he is often called upon for protection in magic spell-castings.

The Loa himself avoids the company of positive god entities and enemies of the demons.

Extremely cruel Loa are not called, but just appeased with sacrificial offerings that are left for them in the forest. This applies also to Bakulu-Baka, who never carries out a possession unless called.

The Mondonge-Mussai-Loa, gods who came from the Congo area, achieved a dubious fame in the Voodoo cult. They demand live dogs as offerings, and bite off their ears to suck out their blood. If such a Loa demands a dog as a sacrifice, Voodoo followers usually feel obligated to fulfill his request, since otherwise he will find a human victim from within the family.

The most-feared female Loa is Marinette-bwa-chéche. She is considered the right hand of the sorcerer-spirit Kita, and the spouse of the cannibalistic Jean-Zandor. She appears as a barn-owl, and the ones possessed by her imitate the creature in all details. Her cult exists only in some areas of Haiti. When she is hunting humans at night, she quickly transforms herself into a werewolf. Her followers are mostly werewolves who consider her their ruler. Voodoo followers believe that werewolves are always female. Ceremonies in honor of Marinette are held solely to appease the Loa with offerings so that she will give up the hunt for humans. The ritual takes place in the forest, where a big fire is built into which the possessed throw themselves. While they are trampling down the fire and the Loa are telling—through their voices—about Marinette's atrocities, the other participants present her with a black chicken, goats, and sometimes also a mother-pig. The sacrificial offerings are buried in the ground so that Marinette can fetch them for herself during the night—she does not like to share with the other Loa.

Marassa

One of the peculiarities of the Voodoo cult is its worship of twins. They inhabit a powerful place next to the Loa that can be traced back to African customs. The special recognition that all living and dead twins enjoy rests on the belief in the divine twins Lisa and Mawu, who represent the male-active and female-passive energies, embodied in sun and moon. Together they are often worshiped as a hermaphrodite-like godly being, an indivisible cosmic unity. Twins are therefore considered their earthly representatives, especially if they are a boy (Dossou) and a girl (Dossa). Africa's Bantu-speaking tribes even permitted twins to marry since they had after all already lain together in their mother's womb. The cult of twins has its likeness in the worship of transsexuals in antiquity, and also among Asian and Indian peoples.

≪≪ MARASSA – DOSSOU – DOSSA ⟶⟩⟩

Loa Marassa is the ruler of all living and dead twins. His symbols are two eggs as a sign of fertility, and crossed V-signs that represent the double gender. In some areas, the twin-Loa is worshiped as the mightiest of all entities. A possession by this Loa at ceremonies seldom takes place. When it does, the possessed person conducts himself in a childlike, unconcerned, or naughty manner, and is fed baby food and poultry by the onlookers.

In any event, the birth of twins arouses much excitement, since they are considered especially powerful beings. They are also looked upon as difficult, irascible, malicious, and extremely sensitive. It is said of most twins that they hate each other, especially if they are identical twins. The belief is that they sometimes try to kill each other in the womb, in order to reunite their divided soul. With a mixed pair, the brother usually suppresses his sister and impedes her development.

The cult of twins serves primarily to curb damage by keeping these mighty entities in good spirits. The children are always watched closely by their relatives so that they cannot harm each other nor their parents. Every family with twins—no matter whether they are alive or dead—is obligated to sacrifice to them.

Traditionally, three pitchers are used to do this. They are tied together (see sketch on the left): two for the twins and one for the Loa Marassa. They receive sacrifices until they make their satisfaction known.

In daily life, it is very important that both children are treated equally or they will react strongly. Families of twins are continually affected by illnesses and accidents, and the followers of Voodoo ascribe this

to the negligence of their duties towards Marassa. It happens sometimes that the twins jealously turn against their parents and put a
powerful spell on them that usually manifests in a mysterious illness.
If such a deed is detected, a Voodoo priest issues a punishment that
the children must bear until they swear to remove the spell from the
afflicted parent.

If one of the twins dies, it is customary for the living twin to
save one half of the food and half
of all the presents he receives.
This custom has its root in
the Yoruba country in
Nigeria. There, an Ibeji figure
takes the place of the
deceased. (The god of twins,
Ibeji is often represented as
two small children.) If the
child was still small when it
died, its parents had to
continue to feed,
clothe, bathe, and
carry around the
Ibeji figure in its
place. It is treated
exactly like the
child that has
survived. The
sketch on the
right shows a
young African
woman who
carries the
Ibeji-figures of
two dead twins

and their ancestral ghosts like children in a cloth.

The followers of Voodoo don't look at twins as the harbingers of misfortune. The danger derives primarily from a misuse of their power. In cases of illness, well-meaning twins are often begged for help, because most of them possess great powers of healing. In addition, the gift of prediction and the ability to influence rain is ascribed to them.

Ritual Possession

Possession is the release of one's own body in order to enable another being to manifest and communicate through it. Since two souls can never abide in one body simultaneously, the possessed must leave his soul, so-to-speak, behind. A possession can last for different lengths of time, from only a few seconds to several hours.

Followers of Voodoo are desirous of this state; it is deliberately brought about. In Africa and Haiti, the possessed are called "horses," and the gods who take possession of their bodies "riders." As we have seen, possession-taking by a Loa is preceded by a religious trance that is induced through rhythmic drum beating and wild dancing, sometimes also through the offering of blood sacrifices. In addition, care is taken that the surroundings will also influence the psyche, through the use of a sacred place, ritual objects, torches, and hearths. Similar practices can be found all over the world, as, for instance, with the war dances of Native Americans and South-Sea islanders, and at Hindu festivals where followers in trance inflict injuries on themselves without pain, piercing their cheeks and tongue.

When a participant in a ritual falls into trance, he suddenly loses mastery over his body. He rolls his eyes and begins to shake uncontrollably, finally becoming unconscious. Shortly after that, a Loa takes the body of the "human horse," entering into his head. The person's expression and conduct change immediately; he is no longer seen as a human being but as the embodiment of a god. The appropriate appurtenances, such as clothing and characteristic accessories, are held ready for the Loa, so that he can suitably present himself.

In the condition of possession, the body is almost invulnerable. Thus, "horses" that are ridden by Damballah (page 43) can let themselves drop head-on from a tree without suffering harm. Others push themselves with all their might against the tip of a sharp sword, or take poisonous drinks, and the ones possessed by a fire god may jump into the fire without burning themselves.

All Loa in Haiti are carefully categorized so it is immediately clear to the Voodoo priest and the participants in a ceremony which god they are confronted with. This fact and the presence of numerous believers provide a certain protection for the possessed individual, because everyone makes sure that the person doesn't suffer any harm.

Likewise, everyone watches to prevent the possessed from getting into any potentially hazardous situations from which he cannot free himself after the Loa has left him: for instance, when Damballah has driven him high up into a treetop or he has dived with Yemaya deep into the ocean. For this purpose, the priest prepares certain offerings that are meant to lure the Loa back to the ceremonial place.

The possessed seldom suffers real injury. True danger issues only from the evil Loa, who do not appear, in most cases, without specific invocation.

The followers of Voodoo who willingly make themselves available for possession try to direct the condition somewhat so that a Loa does not get complete command over their bodies. This is possible, but it requires ritual cleansing and some practice, which must take place under the supervision of a priest. The state of possession is absolutely desirable for the followers, as it transforms them for a short time into one of the gods they worship.

When a Loa has left the one he was riding, the person cannot remember anything that he did while in the trance. This is because all the acts he carried out during the possession, and all messages that he conveyed, took place while his soul was absent. He was at that time in a boundless void, in the spaceless and timeless ether.

The Initiation

The voluntary initiation is usually preceded by an unexpected encounter with a god or a spirit. This often happens during an illness, through an accident, or in the course of some other life crisis that brings about a different state of consciousness. Sometimes it has been known to happen during a dream. This change in the person's vibrational balance is a precondition for establishing contact with other forms of existence and consciousness. A possession does not therefore always take place with the person's consent.

When the one who is called enters a changed consciousness, the entity appears, presenting himself as her guardian spirit. From now on, the spirit makes a certain claim to the body of the new member. On the one hand, this provides the person a certain protection, since she cannot be possessed by another entity without the consent of her guardian spirit. On the other hand, this condition is a lifelong dependency, and the person cannot develop further than the entity who accompanies her. Any too-close nexus with a god or spirit eventually leads into dependency and inhibits the free development of the mind. This certainly is not desirable to someone who seriously aims at perfecting herself.

It is, of course, the person's choice as to whether she wants to enter into a symbiotic relationship with a supernatural being. But the spirit will seek outright a person that corresponds to him and possesses similar characteristics and ethical values. So, the gods who possess the followers during Voodoo ceremonies are revealing a great deal about the character of their "horse."

Shortly after the initiation, a difficult phase begins for the chosen one, during which she must learn to limit involuntary possession. This could have life-threatening consequences, if, for instance, the Loa were to force itself onto her while she was at the wheel of a car.

If the individual wants to survive this period, she must practice mastering her spirit so that she can turn her consciousness on and off as she pleases. Voodoo priests refer to this relationship in the insecure phase as a kind of "wild union."

Human and spirit begin to get used to each other through the ritual of head washing. A thick paste is made from botanical food items and beverages and wrapped in palm leaves, which are then tied to the person's head. A time follows during which the person goes into retreat and fasts. This first phase extends over three days. She is supported by the chants and prayers of other followers. She can then be admitted to a congregation, although she is still regarded as a "wild one."

Only after a series of further exercises and purifications, does she slowly rise in rank. She will gradually get to know all the details about her Loa. On the highest level of the initiation, she undergoes a rebirth that is to free her from old patterns of thought and behavior.

2.

Spirit Servants

Fetishes

A fetish is an object that is inhabited by a spirit. It can be an artificially created object, such as a statue, or parts of animals or plants. Other receptacles, too, that have a hollow space, are suitable for the fetching and keeping of spirits. Remember the well-known tale about the genie in the lamp?

A sorcerer can force or trick a spirit to enter such a receptacle through magnetic invocations, substances, and symbols. In this manner, nature spirits and also the ghosts of ancestors and astral zombies are caught and enslaved.

The entities that inhabit a fetish are able to perform different tasks according to their stage of development. Shamans often use such auxiliary spirits for purposes of healing. In these cases, the shaman works with the positive aspects of the entity and knows how to enhance them. They keep the spirit in a good mood by making offerings and providing other services. The shaman is fully aware that he bears a certain responsibility. He has to take care that the spirit in his custody will not suffer any harm, and he must plan for the future care of the spirit in the event that he should die. If a fetish falls into the wrong hands and the spirit is misused, the shaman must take karmic responsibility and will need to deal with this in his next life.

The drawing on the right pictures the receptacle of a protective spirit who served a witch from Cornwall, England. It consists of the vertebra of an ox, whose unusual shape was probably the reason for using it in this manner.

The sketch on the right shows a fetish figure from Zaire. It has a space inside that can be locked, as do most African items of this sort. It is not known what spirit once inhabited it.

Unfortunately, much misuse takes place with captured spirits: Black-magic practitioners offer blood to them and enrage them by putting nails into the fetish. Then, they set the spirit onto their victim to kill him. However, the more they misuse the spirit in this way, the mightier it becomes. At first, the spirit will ask more and greater sacrifices—frequently from the family of the black-magic practitioner—until finally it has complete mastery over its tormentor, who then himself becomes the slave.

A fetish figure is not always inhabited by a strange spirit entity: A high magician is perfectly able to create and animate such a being with the help of the elements. This spirit is called an elemental.

When dealing with fetishes, each sorcerer has a choice about which energies and powers he wants to work with and have around him. Objects from nature that are specially noticeable due to their shape—or that build a connection with certain spirit beings—are all suitable for magical work. Parts of animals, seeds of plants, unusually shaped stones, are among them. They can be left in their natural energetic state or be magically charged by the sorcerer.

Antelope Fetish

A shaman from Ghana used the natural magical power of this stuffed antelope skull (illustration to the left) to increase his energies. The ornaments were attached to convey an impression of life. The antelope is considered the carrier of messages between the worlds; its characteristics are swiftness and dexterity.

Lamb Fetish

The two-headed lamb (below) comes from the herd of a British witch. Like most oddities of nature, it has unusual energy that sorcerers like to use. The object as such does not tell anything about the possibilities for its use; these were just left to the ingenuity of its owner.

Necklace Fetish

This necklace of a Native American of the Dakota tribe (picture on the right) is made of ermine pelts and the claws of a bear. Little bells, attached to it, facilitate contact with the world of spirits. Its owner connected himself through this necklace with the characteristics of two powerful totem animals whose abilities he wanted to use for his own development. The bear develops strength from deep self-knowledge. Its calm unites itself in this necklace with the ermine's quick apprehension. The ermine sees through situations and connections like a flash, and since it can see behind the masks, it cannot be fooled.

Elementals

Before you decide to create an elemental, you need to be aware that you are responsible for the elemental's actions, just as you are for your own. If, for any reason, whether due to your own fault or not, you lose your control over the elemental, it will affect your fate accordingly.

Begin by making a list of the tasks that you want the elemental to fulfill. Then choose a name, the gender, and the form. The latter could be a simple geometric figure—for instance, a sphere, a cube, or a pyramid. It could just as well be the figure of an animal—there are no limits here to your fantasy. Then select the element with which the being is to be equipped—fire, water, earth, or air—produce it and stow it. It should be tuned as closely as possible to the task and form of the elemental. An advanced magician can also create an elemental that combines the attributes of all four elements.

Once the tasks are listed, you need to determine how much time it will take to carry out each one. An elemental moves independent of time and space, and so it can accomplish its task with the speed of lightning. Then you need to decide on a command upon which it must return to its body. It is also extremely important to set a fixed life span, exact as to year, day, and hour, and also by what command this is to happen, and how the end will take place. A proven method is the backward-spelling of the name and the willful dissolution into its elements.

Beside wiping out the elemental, there is another way to get rid of it. When the predetermined time has arrived for the elemental to take its leave, you can give it into the custody of a higher spirit or elementary being. This trade must of course have been arranged beforehand with care.

To repeat: It is of great importance to lay down all of this, because elementals have a tendency to develop a personal life. They often orient themselves along the character traits of the magician who created them, and frequently they distinctly favor his undesirable traits. The longer you work with elementals, the stronger they become, since they are again and again charged with energy. If such a being should outlive you, its creator, remember that you will remain responsible beyond your death for the elemental's deeds.

The Creation of an Elemental

Choose as simple an object as possible. Then, with your concentrated will, call the elemental out from the cosmos and *imagine* it into the object. Choose carefully the hour that is governed by the element. If the being is to work for you, charge it through your own body. That means you first collect the element's energy in your body and then conduct it by the strength of your will through your fingers and into the object.

To make sure that the charge is sufficient, hold a pendulum over it; its oscillations will indicate the strength of the energy. Test to see whether the charged object feels cold, warm, or hot, according to the chosen element. Before your inner eye, a fire elemental will appear as a red triangle, a water elemental as a whitish sphere, an earth elemental as an earth clod, and an air elemental as a bluish-greenish sphere.

When you have accomplished this task satisfactorily, give the being its chosen name—without it, nothing is possible. Say the name loudly three times and, with it "Live! Live! Live!" Go on to program the being with the attributes it should have, so that you can confer a spell and transfer images and sensations onto it. Then, give it a clearly stated task and let it know the time span in which it is to be carried out. Determine the word or gesture that lets the elemental immediately return into the object assigned to him. After that, establish the lifetime of your creation and decide when it shall die or be handed on.

After the elemental has left its body, cut the nexus between it and yourself, so that it can move freely. That happens either before your inner eye or with scissor-steel cuts of energy. Then consciously turn your attention to other things. On the established date, check to see if the elemental has returned into its body, using the pendulum test described above. If the elemental has not yet been able to fulfill its task, call it back with the chosen command and repeat the magic charging until you achieve a satisfactory result. When you repeat the process, keep in mind that you should not overburden the being with too many different tasks, and that a clear delineation of the goal brings faster results and is easier to check.

The Light Elemental

A light elemental is comparatively easy to create, and most of the time it is given only one ability. This procedure is preferred for purposes of healing, to obtain desired abilities of all sorts, or to fill particular areas with success, good fortune, and more. An elemental may be created for your own aims or for those of others.

First, determine the task that the creature shall fulfill, and its name and form. Then imagine an ocean of light. Dip your hands into it and lift out some of the light substance. Form a sphere out of it in front of your body and gradually enlarge it by adding more and more of the light substance. Press the energy together well until you feel its power. When the sphere has reached the circumference of a big ball, begin giving it the desired form.

Once this is completed, you may want to baptize the elemental while calling it by name three times. Then tell it the task it is to carry out and for whom, and state the time by which the task should be fulfilled. Order the elemental to return to the ocean of light when it has finished its job. Finally, with a forceful motion, hurl the creature back into the cosmos and tear or cut apart the energetic band that is connecting you with the creature. You can do this purely in your imagination or you may want to use a pair of scissors or a knife. Then, immediately start a different activity.

It is extremely important that you release the elemental, since only then can it fulfill its task without being impeded. Whenever you spiritually occupy yourself with it, the elemental will immediately return to its environment. If the goal is not met by a certain time, call the creature back and charge it anew with energy from the ocean of light.

Elementals that are created in this manner are very effective and well equipped to use the attributes assigned to them, independent of your own abilities.

The Soul Doll

We are dealing here with a Voodoo technique for the creation of a golem, an artificial and enlivened creature, which is also called an elemental. Elementals are created in all cultures, but different procedures are followed. This creation too carries a certain risk, since the creature over time tends to develop a life of its own that is not under your control. The creation of a soul doll carries tremendous responsibility.

The first step must therefore be the determination of its life span. It is important to couple it with your own death, so that it then will also die or become the possession of another person who is named at the time of its creation.

As a base, the soul doll receives your attributes, positive and negative. Therefore, it's important that you have sufficient information about yourself, especially about your weaknesses.

You need to meditate for three days in front of a mirror about the looks that the doll is to have. It is important that it resemble you, that it have your physical characteristics. It is up to you whether you include your physical shortcomings in your creation.

Then, obtain fabric in a favorite color or in the color you want for the doll. Of course, water is also necessary—water, for instance, from a rainwater barrel or a brook—into which you mix some of your favorite perfume and your own urine. Wash the fabric in the water and bathe it on three consecutive days. Now, on the first night, place the fabric under your head and neck; on the following night, under your chest; then under your stomach; and finally under your pelvis, so that the fabric takes up your energies.

Next, choose the place where the doll is to be made. It should be a quiet place in which normally no other activity is carried out. Work on the doll only when you're feeling well and in good spirits, so that you can charge it with the greatest amount of positive energy.

Once you've determined the size of the doll, draw its outline onto the fabric; front and back, two parts only. Limbs and head may never be attached individually and the head may not be separated from the torso by a seam.

Sew the doll together and fill it. The classic filling materials are tea leaves and bones—in any case, natural materials. If you use parts from other living beings (bones, hairs), make sure the parts have your characteristics. Use your imagination in creating the doll's inner organs, but here are some ideas:

The heart may be made of clay, or you could insert a small red bag in the approximate place. Your own hair might fill the head; a fish bone could be used as the spine. The lungs can be small balloons filled with your own breath; the kidneys little balls drenched in urine; and the intestines simply a cord. Arms and legs can also contain your hair, and for the hands and feet your own nails would be suitable. There are no limits to your fantasy.

It is important to the creation of the doll that it be agreeable to you and have a pleasant appearance, so here once more you need to take special care. Woolen thread, a piece of a fur, or a doll's wig might be used for hair. Its eyes, eyebrows, nose, and mouth, depending on your skill, can be painted on, stitched on, or applied from different materials (felt, buttons, fish teeth, crystals, etc.). Its ears could consist of small shells or pieces of wood. You can buy plastic toenails and fingernails for pasting-on, or you could insert small crystals. Finally, dress the doll as you would like to dress yourself. Outfit it with shoes, handbag, jewelry if appropriate, perfume or cologne, and all important accessories. It should also have money in its pocket.

While you are working on the doll, protect it well. Wrap it in white silk fabric and store it in a safe place so that the energy you put into it doesn't get lost. When the doll is completed, give it a name, which you must keep secret under all circumstances. Call its name three times, adding: "Live! Live! Live!" Then put the doll back in its white silk cloth. Repeat this procedure on nine consecutive days. The period of the waxing moon is the best time to do this.

At this point, the doll no longer needs to be completely hidden and guarded; nevertheless, it is better not to talk about the things that you do with it. Put it in a secure spot, and place next to it something to drink and a candle. Speak with it and treat it respectfully. The doll is now able to carry out certain duties.

If you want healing powers, you must request them and give the doll the corresponding order. The soul doll is also capable of acting in your place. If you need money, give it some coins and ask it to multiply them. The possibilities of its services are boundless.

If the doll should get lost or be destroyed, you need to positively separate yourself from it with a ritual, since it contains parts of your soul. Bathe in salt water, rinse your mouth with alcohol, shave off all your body hair, put on new clothes, and temporarily assume a new name. In addition, consciously draw back into yourself that part of your soul that lived in the doll. Repeat this ritual until you are totally sure that all your energies have returned to you. You will feel it.

Yidam

A yidam is an elemental that is created in a far-eastern manner, though, actually, this practice is known to only a few magicians there. The preparations are the same ones used in the creation of other elementals. It is important to determine the creature's life span to the hour. After you have precisely determined all its important attributes and capabilities, you can begin with the creation process.

The ritual is traditionally performed outdoors in a lonely, remote place. Lay out the necessary symbols with stones.

Choose first a symbol or sign that is to characterize the elemental. Then, on a big square paper box, draw a large circle in red to represent the all-embracing ether.

Draw two squares into it that overlap, forming an octagon (see the sketch to the left).

Draw the symbol of the elemental in the center, also in red. The form must be large enough so that the creature has plenty of space around it. Such a picture is called a "great kylichor" in Tibet.

For the small kylichor (sketch to the right), you need a small metal plate made from gold, silver, copper, or some other metal. Engrave the symbol of the creature on it with a pointed implement. With the small kylichor, you can call the yidam whenever it is needed, either by a gesture or a word that has been determined in advance. Always store the small kylichor in a safe place or carry it on your body.

Place the small kylichor on the symbol in the middle of the large kylichor, while calling out the name of the yidam. Then, sit comfortably and begin breathing into your body the element of fire (see the chapter "Magic Exercises") until you distinctly feel its attributes—heat and heaviness. When you are completely filled with that element, transfer the total energy into your fingers or aura (see "Bodies of Light") and focus it on the little metal plate. Press the energy together into a tiny spark and place the attributes, with concentrated will, into the element that the yidam will later have at its disposal. Repeat this procedure seven times, enlarging the elemental each time by the size of a spark.

When the creature has reached the desired size, use your imagination to form the flame you have created into the desired shape. If, during this process, your concentration weakens, send the creature to the place that is to be his abode—a wall, a stone, a figurine, etc. Hide the small and the large kylichor; roll them together in silk or fold them and store them securely. Next time, you can simply unfold both and call the creature to you.

An elemental can, of course, also be created out of any one of the four elements. If the yidam is to be made from earth, imagine an ocean of earth from which you form your creature clot by clot. If you want to use water, dam up the power in a drop, whose volume increases. For the element of air, choose a cloud.

After the completion of the yidam, you can charge it even further to increase its power. This procedure is always carried out with the large kylichor. To call the creature to give him an order, you will from now on take out only the little metal plate that you wear most of the time on a chain around your neck.

Yidams that have been created in this way can develop into very powerful entities that become so strong that they can be perceived even by uninitiated people. These creatures tend to develop their own personalities, in line with your own specific characteristics. For this reason, you need to pay special attention to your own ethical development, and refrain from giving them orders for which they would have to destroy something. You must also always insist on the execution of your orders, so that you retain control over the element.

In Tibet, yidams are often employed for the protection of the magician and for the healing of the sick. Other elementals can move objects from one location to another or relay messages. The yidam may have greater abilities than you do. But you are the one who decides upon the kind of powers it will have. If you are clever, you will give your yidam only one task at a time—and not too many different ones—because the results will be better. At the end of the creature's already determined life span, dissolve it into its elements and tear up and burn the large kylichor.

Zombies

The creation of zombies, more than any other practice, has given a bad name to the followers of Voodoo; it involves a form of black magic that originated in Africa, from which it also takes its name: Zombie is Congolese and means "enslaved spirit." The practice is, fortunately, very rare.

The bokor (black magic practitioner) begins by magically killing his victim, generating—or faking—a regular, temporary brain death. He forces his victim's soul into a vessel to train it for use as a demon. If the person was buried, the magician will disinter and revive him. If he succeeds, the body he gets has no will of its own and will carry out each of his orders. If the bokor does not succeed in reviving his victim's body, he is left with the captured soul, which is called an astral zombie. Astral zombies, again, are not exclusive to the African-Haitian Voodoo cult, but also are used in other magic cults.

Zombies act and move like machines. They are usually put to work in the fields, where they function like slaves for their masters. To avoid their being recognized by members of their family, they are moved to faraway places and worked during the night.

Only a very high-ranking magician can bring a zombie back into the realm of the living (see page 282, "Bringing Back Zombies"). He combines the material and the energetic bodies by means of the electromagnetic energies of the cosmos. A zombie whose family finds him and brings him home normally dies a short time later. In order to free the soul, it is essential to find the vessel in which the bokor confined it. This vessel must then be opened and destroyed.

Capturing and holding too many souls and spirit creatures has brought many a magician to his doom. If they get together and revolt against their captor, his power is rarely sufficient to deter them when they attack and cannibalize him.

Magic with Spirit Servants

The Sending of Dead

If a person wants to inflict death by consumption on his enemy, he orders a bokor who can activate a so-called "sending of dead." It causes the victim to undergo rapid weight loss, to cough blood, and finally to succumb to the tremendous loss of strength. This form of black magic is greatly feared by followers of Voodoo. It leads to death within a few days.

The magician first obtains the agreement of the specific death demon. To get it, he goes to a cemetery at night and pounds three times with a machete against the black stone cross that belongs to Baron Samedi (see the chapter "The Loa—Gods of Voodoo"). The bokor sacrifices some black animals in the Baron's honor, and adds pieces of potato, which symbolize the bleaching-out—the elimination—of the intended victim.

After he receives a sign that his offerings have been accepted, he takes a few handfuls of earth from the cemetery, puts them in his satchel and takes them along. At home, he places on his altar a statue of St. Expedit, the guardian or patron saint of "expeditions." Then he calls out a curse asking the saint to destroy the enemy and let the dead rise from their graves, so that they can invade the body and soul of the enemy and consume them.

Finally, the bokor strews some of the earth from the cemetery before the victim's door. He also distributes it on the street where the victim will be walking. In this manner, he marks a trail that the dead can easily follow. Once they locate the unsuspecting person, they invade him and begin to nourish themselves with his vital energies. The victim's body and soul deteriorate frighteningly fast after that, and he is carried to his grave a few days later.

It is by no means certain that the spirits who invade the victim are the souls of dead persons. Strange ghostly creatures and poltergeists do many kinds of mischief—for instance, using peoples' remains by inhabiting parts of corpses that have not yet totally decomposed—in order to be able to influence earthly matter through them. Many shamans are not at all aware of the entities with whom they keep company, an ignorance that is to their disadvantage when they have to pay for their deeds. Everything has its price.

Demonic Magic

Probably the most repulsive form of magic that is even now practiced in Africa and Haiti, is demonic magic. It is mentioned here in order to inform people affected by it about the cause of their pain, so that they can take countermeasures.

As is true in many other cases of bad magic, some magicians and their patrons do not take into consideration that they are working with unreliable and uncontrollable spirit entities who are often insatiable and will not hold to any agreements. The demons are called bakas, and they can, if necessary, appear as dogs, cats, cows, and other domestic animals. Bakas are not necessarily from hell. Lost souls from the transitional realm, such as the suddenly deceased or suicides, belong to this group, as do spirits who have not yet found the road to the realm of the dead. It also happens that such confused and disappointed spirits are trained by a magician to commit atrocities.

A poorly informed patron is frequently deceived by the bokor and demon, about the price of this work. If a baka receives the order to kill a man, it expects as payment the sacrifice of a person who belongs to the patron's family. Since these demons sustain themselves through peoples' suffering and pain, they are of course anxious to have it last for a long time. Again and again they approach the magician and the patron, making new claims.

If the patron agrees that the execution of the order will cost him "only two chickens," it means that the demon will fetch two of his children. Even if the patron was tricked and agreed to this unknowingly, it is too late. Unfortunately, it still happens that family members are thrown as "feed" to the demons out of the pure greed of one of their "loved ones."

Bokors who work with such demons are usually of a sadistic nature and covetous of power. In the traditional Voodoo cult, human sacrifices are considered highly objectionable and are appropriately punished. Black-magic sorcerers who use such practices are therefore the exception, but they have brought Voodoo into worldwide disrepute. A Voodoo priest who has reached the desired developmental level never needs to dive so low; he knows other ways to keep enemies within bounds.

Serpent Magic

Sometimes, on their return from a visit to Africa or the Caribbean, people die of a mysterious "tropical illness." The following information may serve to illuminate the background.

The bokor obtains a snake, which he kills as slowly as possible. While it is still alive, he draws blood from it that he mixes with earth from the cemetery. He lets this mixture dry and later puts a pinch into the victim's food. A few days later, the victim falls ill, because his veins are full of numerous tiny snakes.

Dog Magic

This invoked magic with animal spirits is sent in a dream. It is used mostly to spur a man to carry out a certain deed, such as canceling or fulfilling a contract, or collecting debts.

To accomplish this, the bokor fills a dog's skull with a paste of various herbs and pieces of bone, and ties it closely (see sketch above). Next, he lets chicken blood flow over it, which attracts the appropriate dog spirits and lends them the power to manifest on the level of dreams. After the bokor has laid a track to the victim's home, he buries the skull either beside the victim's house or along a road that the victim travels daily.

The victim will now be plagued by nightmares until he has acted as the sorcerer and his patron desire. In his nightly nightmares, he is attacked by wild dogs who inflict not only psychological but physical damage as well. Cursed in this manner, he wakes up with very painful bite wounds.

The Sending of Nightmares

Another way to send nightmares that may cause physical injury is through the action of a particular demon named Cauquemere. This creature was adopted from the Central American Indian tribes and is in direct contact with the spirit of the werewolf (see the chapter "Demons, Elemental Spirits, Sphere Creatures"). Understandably, extreme caution is essential in any contact with him. Possession must be prevented at any cost.

The ritual is held at night because that is when Cauquemere works. For it, the sorcerer needs a handheld mirror and a photo of the victim. He places the picture in front of the mirror and draws behind it the vèvès of the Gédé family and of the Petro-Loa. In addition, he places two black candles on each side. For his own protection, the arrangement is densely encircled with salt. He burns incense with ivy, resin, and stinging nettle leaves. Once the smoke has risen, he lights the candles. The sorcerer then points his magic wand toward the mirror and murmurs the demon's name continuously and monotonously while he carefully observes the mirror. When the magic wand begins vibrating and a dark shadow appears in the mirror, he can assume that Cauquemere has arrived. Then the conjuring begins. It sounds like this or something similar:

Cauquemere, this is the image of my enemy, who deserves just punishment...(name). Cauquemere, to torture...(name) in the following seven nights with the worst dreams, I permit you to leave the door of the mirror. He shall writhe in pain, fear, and illness. Cauquemere, I order you to return into your world after fulfilling your task, and this door will close.

Thank you for your services. Be it so!

The formula is repeated until the creature leaves and has taken up the track. The mirror then is clear again, and the stream of energy in the wand dries up. In order not to owe anything to the spirit—which could happen, especially if sending Cauquemere was not justified—the magician places a piece of red meat on a plate in the circle as a sacrifice.

At dawn, when Cauquemere has returned to his world, the mirror is wrapped in black silk for protection and sealed with the sign of Legba. It is easy to remove the cloth again in the evening so that the demon can continue his work.

The circle of salt remains during the entire ritual. After seven days the vèvès are destroyed at daybreak. For safety's sake, incense is burned and the sacrificial gifts are carried off. Should the presence of Cauquemere still be noticeable the following night, the mirror is also destroyed and thrown away the next day.

The Hand of the Dead Man

This magic stems from a European witchcraft tradition. Needed for it was a hand cut off a hanged man (the hand had to be taken while the corpse was still hanging). The hand was dried or roasted over a fire. Next, a candle was attached to the hand, or the fingers of the hand were dipped in oil beforehand so they could serve as a candle. In this way, the sorcerer created for himself a kind of "handyman," who was able to carry out different magical orders.

It is generally very simple to achieve results with this kind of corpse-desecration magic, since a direct connection to the realm of the dead is established through the relic. But be warned: these practices often take on a life of their own, for with them the magician is personally addressing the spirit of the dead. The spirit doesn't have to be the ghost of the deceased himself, but might be a ghost creature that took possession of the corpse shortly after death in order to exert influence on a material level. It may also be a so-called poltergeist. In both cases, to work with such creatures is undoubtedly dangerous and could possibly get out of control. Even the ghost of an upright man would sooner or later attempt to free itself from a sorcerer's power. It is not rare for the sorcerer to end up being ruled by the spirit he evoked, especially if he has been working with the spirit for a long time and supplied it with much energy. In the worst case scenario, he might finally be destroyed by the creature.

From an ethical standpoint, it is in any event, unjustifiable to force the spirit of a deceased person to remain close to the earthly sphere. That would be hampering its further development, which in turn would unfavorably affect the sorcerer's fate.

3.
Doll Magic

Although Voodoo dolls are generally associated with Haitian Voodoo cults, this form of magic has a long tradition in many countries.

The Voodoo doll in Sulawesi (Indonesia), for instance, is life-size, which helps to stimulate the sorcerer's imagination so that he is better able to affect his victim's body. In Haiti, Hungary, Russia, and the South Seas, dolls the size of children's toys are used. Old practices of Western witchcraft used candles instead of dolls, or worked with both. For some African witches, a doll serves as an image of their goddess and forms the core of their altar.

Known all over the world, doll magic is generally taken quite seriously. This facilitates their use, since the collective unconscious is open to such magic, and the unconscious of the individual can easily be reached.

In witchcraft with Voodoo dolls, a mini-situation is created that is to influence the large one ("As in the microcosm, so in the macrocosm"), in accordance with the spiritual order that lies behind such magic.

Voodoo dolls can be employed for many purposes, but always with the aim of affecting a human being. How this magic is used will, in any case, affect the practitioner's fate. Extreme caution is warranted, especially with harmful magic that might bring illness or death. Only if the victim has a great deal of evil in himself, or has committed despicable acts that justify such a procedure, can witchcraft become effective in the manner intended. The victim need not believe in the effectiveness of witchcraft or magic to be vulnerable to it. Of course, the effectiveness of any act of witchcraft depends upon the honest intention behind it and the sensitive intensity with which the ritual is carried out. But even though an unconscious fear may trigger the desired effect in the victim, the sorcerer can count on experiencing strong repercussions for causing harm to others, including accidents, illnesses, or even death.

There are no limits to the choice of materials your imagination can come up with for making Voodoo dolls. Originally, they were made out of clay: the hollow body was filled with the victim's hairs, fingernails, or body secretions in order to connect the figure even more strongly with the sorcerer's energy. Such charging is desirable, but not absolutely necessary to the success of the magic. Dolls sewn from fabric are very popular, since they can easily be filled with various materials. Basically, all natural materials, such as wood, straw, or wax, are suitable for making a doll. Most important is that it have a close similarity to the targeted person or bear his or her characteristics, which could be expressed by clothing or physical form. If necessary, you can attach a photo of the person to the figure.

After it is completed, you need to "enliven" the doll in a ritual: With the help of a straw, you can give it the breath of life through mouth and nose. Then call it three times by name, and you may want to baptize it. These preparations may deviate slightly from culture to culture, but all rest on one basic principle: the doll is a close image of the intended victim magically enlivened in order to function as a substitute.

Here are some of the ways this magic is carried out in different parts of the world.

Love Magic

Love magic that is performed with a Voodoo doll will certainly bring the couple together. Nevertheless, this witchcraft too should be carried out with a high sense of responsibility. It works best when the desired partner has already shown interest, but for some reason doesn't quite dare to take the initiative, or is afraid of becoming emotionally attached. Other seemingly superficial obstacles can also be removed in this manner.

If, however, the desire is to force another individual into a relationship, it will not bring true love to either side. It is possible that the chosen partner may turn his attention to the male or female witch. Yet such forced relationships are usually of short duration. You can never be sure of your partners' love, since they have not entered into it out of their free will.

A woman who is desirous of a man, forms two dolls out of clay—one of herself, and one of the man she loves. She furnishes them with gender characteristics, and fills them, if possible, with some hairs and fingernails. Next, she ties them together with a string—better yet with a red silk ribbon. Their posture should simulate the love act.

It is best to carry out such a

charm on a Friday in the period of the waxing moon. Friday is dedicated to Venus, the goddess of love, and the waxing moon promotes the attraction. The gods of love (Venus/Aphrodite and Cupid/Eros) can be invoked during the ritual. The spreading of orange blossoms on your altar will have a supportive effect: many cultures consider them wedding flowers. Further devices, designed to enhance the imagination, can be chosen at your discretion and incorporated into the ritual.

When the ritual has ended, wrap the dolls in a silk rose-colored fabric, if possible, and store them in a safe place. You can repeat the procedure several times if needed, during the waxing moon.

If you invoked the charm with honest intentions, success will come soon.

Winning a Court Case

Cover the altar, or whatever place you are using for the ritual (which could also be the ground), with a white cloth. The doll, which, in this case, should be made of cloth, is rubbed with obi oil (a Voodoo product that can be purchased in specialized shops), placed on the cloth, and then sprinkled with verbena.

Tie a white thread around the waist of the doll, which embodies your opponent, and chant the following spell:

Like this I tie my enemy who would speak against me.
Now he is still, and I come free, free, free.

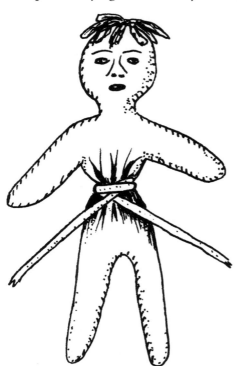

Repeat the tying of the enemy seven times in a row. While you are saying these words, burn an incense mixture of olibanum (frankincense) and myrrh. It is good idea to wear an amulet as you perform the spell, or put on rosemary oil.

When the ritual is complete, wrap the doll in white cloth and hide it in a secret place.

Carry out the spell every day for several days before the trial date, always after sunset. On the last evening, burn the doll after the ritual, together with the white cloth, and scatter the ashes in all directions.

Healing Magic

Make the doll from cloth, and consider it a substitute for the sick person. It can be either the color of the sick one's aura or a neutral white. After the preparations described earlier, stick needles into the doll in the places where the sick individual has pain, while burning a purifying incense like myrrh or immortelle (everlasting flower).

The aim is to transfer the illness from the human body to the doll. The magic works best when carried out during the time of the waning moon. You will need the highest concentration possible. When the ritual has produced an effect, burn the doll and turn its ashes over to running waters, terminating the ups and downs of the sickness.

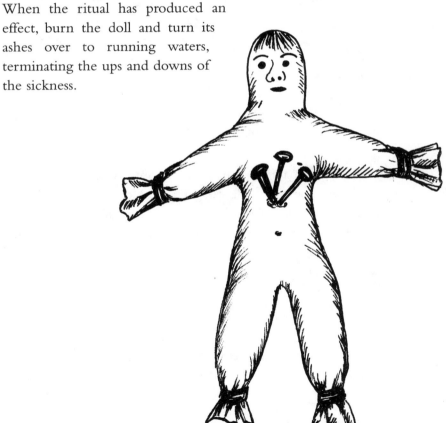

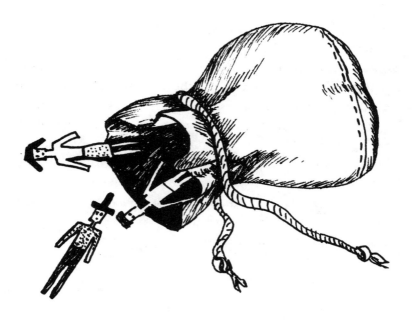

Worry Dolls

This form of doll magic originated in a South American tradition: Indian children use tiny dolls to get rid of their worries. In the evening, before falling asleep, the child tells one of these little dolls her worries and then places it under her pillow. By morning, all the child's worries have been carried off by the fetish. During the day, store the dolls in a cloth bag.

Success Magic

On May Day or All Saints' Day (November 1), fashion a small doll from branches of rosemary. Wrap a green silk ribbon around its arms, legs, and torso. Keep the doll in the kitchen until the evening before the event you're seeking success in. Then put the figure in a glass of wine and drink to the health of the benevolent spirits—those spirits that are in contact with the plant. The doll functions as an aid to the spirits so that it is easier for them to exert influence on the material level.

This ritual, which comes from the Mediterranean region, can also be carried out together with others who are part of the project.

Self-Defense

You can make these dolls of fabric or soft clay. The ritual begins when the doll has reached an agreement—on a magical level—with the attacker. Work in candlelight and ask the spirits for assistance. The manner of proceeding depends on the manner of attack; your fantasy can have no limits.

If you are plagued by defamation of character attacks, stick needles in the doll's mouth to hinder your opponent in spreading lies.

If someone tries to push you out of your job, you might stick needles in the doll's seat. Your competitor will then lose *his* job.

If you're sure that a curse has been inflicted on you, you can return it to the sender with the doll's help. You can, for instance, push pieces of broken glass into a soft clay doll, and give the order that your opponent writhe in pain until the ritual candles have burned out. At the end, remove the shards. This form of Voodoo alerts the enemy to the repercussions from renewed attacks, giving him an unequivocal warning.

There are no ethical objections concerning the practice of this reflective Voodoo magic, since it serves the purpose of self-defense, and its effect only unfolds if it is justified.

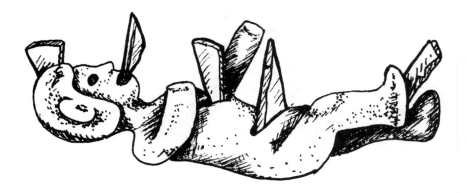

Harmful Magic with Voodoo Dolls

As already described at the beginning of this book, it is advisable to refrain from such forms of magic. An exception exists in extreme cases of self-defense or if someone's life is at stake. In unjust cases, the spell often will not be fully successful; it works best when it is cast in response to a piece of magic that can be reflected back to the sender. This form of Voodoo has fallen into ill repute all over the world, since in many cases serious harm has been inflicted out of envy, ill-will, or low motivations.

Attention:
These descriptions are presented for information only:
it is not recommended that you copy them!

In order to put themselves in the requisite evil mood, some sorcerers use deplorable techniques. In Africa and Haiti, a Voodoo priestess prepares herself for a destruction-ritual by biting off the head of a living chicken and chewing its intestines. Through the energetic vibrations of the violent death of a living creature, the appropriate demons are called, and they can then become most effective with their vicious powers.

In the Europe in earlier times, black magicians would nail toads to a cross with their heads upside-down, for instance, or impale a cat and then burn it. The sorcerer was at this point often close to madness, having stayed in the woods for days on end without food or drink.

It is urgently advised that people refrain from such practices in all cases—they are indefensible. For one thing, the magic becomes uncontrollable through the demons' interference, and for another, the sorcerer harms his own body and soul through his malicious actions. Therefore, once more, I would like to stress that these descriptions are here for informational purposes only and should not be imitated under any circumstances.

The modern witch uses other procedures, if she wants to get spirit creatures to support her work. If she insists on arousing demons, she needs only black candles and the vèvè of the desired spirit. As already mentioned, it is most important for the success of the work for her to put herself in an intuitive state. By doing this, she creates a sphere in which the spirit can act. If sacrifices are demanded, they can be made in form of amulets or other items and food.

A warning: It can become dangerous for the sorceress herself if she has her enemy hounded by a demon. Should the spirit not find sufficient negative energy in its victim, it will turn against those who called it in order to finish its destructive work.

Abasement

For this purpose, the sorceress sews a doll out of black fabric and fills it with organic material. Then she cuts a slit in its back and sprinkles sharp pepper into it. In addition, she writes her victim's name on a piece of paper and slides that into the slit also. Then she closes the opening with a piece of wire, and bends the doll's arms backwards, fastening its hands. This is to make sure that the victim is helpless. Finally, she puts the doll in a kneeling position, facing the wall.

This magic is used to maneuver attackers into a helpless situation and robbing them of their vital energies. Such a spell would be justified only for purposes of self-defense when your own life is threatened.

Destruction

For this spell, the bokor (black magic practitioner) needs a photo and a few hairs of the targeted person. He cuts a human figure from black cardboard and attaches the photo with needle and thread, or tacks it to the heart area of the silhouette; the hairs are glued to the head. Next, the bokor takes the figure to a compost heap or buries it in putrid, muddy ground, while muttering his invocations and curses. As the figure slowly rots away, so the victim loses his vital energy and falls more and more prey to insanity.

Needle Magic

The following destruction-magic comes from Africa. A doll is made out of fabric, straw, or soft clay, bearing the characteristics of the attacker. If possible, the sorceress gets hairs or fingernails of the victim, or something that has picked up the enemy's vital energy, such as a piece of his clothing; best is a fabric item that has been worn. She works something of that into the doll.

After having "enlivened" the doll, the sorceress transports herself into an emotional condition that is suitable for her undertaking—in this case, destructive rage and hate. Then she "shoots" the concentrated, negative emotional load into the doll, while piercing the enemy's image with needles. If the whole body of the doll is pierced in this manner, it leads to the total destruction of the victim.

Physicians are often mystified when they deal with such conditions, since the patient becomes weaker and weaker without a recognizable medical reason, suffering from severe pain and finally dying.

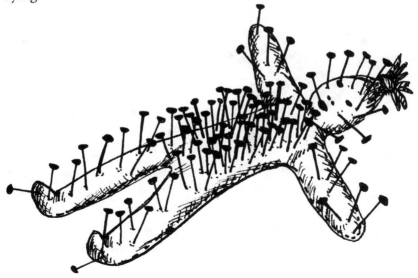

Pain and Death

This ritual is most often carried out during the time of the waning moon. The doll can be fashioned out of wax. At first, the sorcerer sticks needles into various body parts to cause pain to the attacker. In addition, he ties together the doll's arms and legs, so that its help-lessness is evident. As illustrated, a photo is often used in the magic procedure.

When the doll has been tormented enough with needles and ropes, which charges the sorcery with hate and negative energy, it is melted over a fire. The sorcerer focuses, to begin with, on the body part that is supposed to bring death to the attacker. The remains are buried or thrown into running water.

If the sorcerer is deeply convinced that the attacker really deserves to die, and if he was successful in building up many nega-tive feelings, such as hate and fury during the ceremony, the spell will quite certainly have its desired effect.

In another method of sending an enemy to the hereafter, the doll is made out of natural materials. Here, too, needles are inserted in the doll. A stone—heavier than the figure—is fastened to the doll, which is thrown into running waters, where it is supposed to slowly decay. Like the doll, the enemy will slowly waste away, and finally die when the doll is completely destroyed.

Time for Magic

With harmful magic, the right time is of major importance. In general, such magic is best carried out in the time of the waning moon, preferably in an hour governed by Mars. The hours are as follows:

Monday	Tuesday	Wednesday	Thursday	Friday	Saturday	Sunday
04.00	01.00	05.00	02.00	06.00	03.00	07.00
11.00	08.00	12.00	09.00	13.00	10.00	14.00
18.00	15.00	19.00	16.00	20.00	17.00	21.00
	22.00	23.00	00.00			

Red and black garments are often worn during the performance of such magic. Red clothes symbolize vital energy, for one thing; for another, aggression and brutality. Black clothes are useful in protecting the sorcerer from hostile creatures, and in addition, they preserve the secrecy of his doings.

Proven Examples

During his extensive travels in the 20s and 30s, the American journalist William Seabrook often came in contact with magic rites and their victims. Traveling on several continents, he discovered the similarity of occult practices. The following case examples are from his reports:

In the 20s, a young French auto mechanic fell in love with a country girl, much to her grandmother's displeasure. One day he had a sharp quarrel with the old woman. After they parted, he took a walk through the countryside on an easily traversable mountain path. At the same time, the grandmother went into her house to put a spell on him. In her old wine cellar she built a miniature landscape out of thorns and branches of wild roses. Into this thicket she laid a doll in the image of the young man. The doll was chained hand and foot, and its eyes were bandaged. Then she spoke:

> *Confused spirit is going to twist and turn,*
> *and confused foot follows...*
> *Be confused, be confused and twist and turn,*
> *for tangled nets are woven.*

When the man had not yet returned after dark, a search was begun for him. He was found in a thorny thicket near the path, unable to move his legs. He said that he suddenly became dizzy and believed he had suffered a stroke.

Seabrook was certain that this was a case of ritual magic. In order to find proof for his suspicions, he broke into the old woman's cellar. He found the place of ritual and took the doll along with him to show to the young man.

The young man was angry that the old woman had tried to harm him, but did not want to believe that his condition was the result of sorcery. There was no doubt in his mind that he was the victim of his own powerful unconscious imagination, and he refused to recognize the true reason for his paralysis. If he had been able to reconstruct the occurrence consciously, his ailments would have disappeared immediately.

In another occurrence in the 30s, Voodoo magic was increased by "whispering"—the power of suggestion.

A concert pianist was privately very much occupied with occultism through an interest in the Rosicrucians and other magical societies. Eventually he came in contact with a controversial esoteric sect, which, however, he left after a dispute. The angry members of the sect made a doll that they clothed in a tuxedo, like the one the pianist wore on stage. The doll's hands were clamped into a vise that was tightened daily. In addition, sect members who were not known to the pianist started criticizing his performances. Under the cover of being concerned, they asked whether he was perhaps over-working. They were voicing their concern, they claimed, because his playing no longer seemed so fluent. Might he perhaps have contracted an inflammation of the nerves?

This web of magic began to show its effects after a few weeks. The pianist concentrated increasingly on his fingers, and his playing became weaker. Finally, he received an anonymous letter before he was to make an important appearance. The sender mentioned a theory about the magical connection of image and man, a theory of which the pianist was aware. In this letter was also a description of the doll whose hands were clamped into the vise. On the evening of the performance, the pianist received another letter with the following words: "Tonight the vise will slowly tighten until your hands are broken." That night the artist broke down completely and was not able to perform at the concert. After a number of false starts and disharmonies, he fled the stage in embarrassment.

Here, the victim already believed in the power of magic spells and was familiar with their effects. For this reason, his tormentors used—

in addition to magic—the highly effective psychological power of suggestion. With its help, even an openly uttered curse can have an effect. It is not rare that a victim dies through autosuggestion—that is, by injecting himself with these "whisperings"—because he knows that his enemy is using magic rituals against him in order to bring about his death.

4.
Demons,
Elemental Spirits,
Sphere Creatures

Demons

The term "demon" comes from the Greek word *daimon*, which means "god." These beings were seen as very powerful and generally bore a connection to destiny. Originally, they were seen as guardians of justice and executors of fate. Only in Christendom were they defamed as devils who wanted to stop humans from following Christ into the light. This condemnation, however, was only a strategy to get the heathen peoples to give up their old gods. Certain demons have indeed taken on the task of leading men into temptation, but this challenge has a value: it serves the individuals' self-knowledge, since a demon can only hold up a mirror to man.

A demon begins to harm a man only when he finds much wickedness in him, which he then throws back at him multiplied many times. Demons are primarily creatures of justice. A person who knows his weaknesses and admits them has nothing to fear from demons. These creatures despise dissemblers and hypocrites, whom they then attack in an artful way, confronting the pretenders with their own shadow. If individuals are clever enough in this situation to recognize their mistake and master their negative feelings, the demon will lose interest and turn away, since he sees that his task has been fulfilled.

Association with these creatures can, however, take a man to the deepest and least known depths of his soul. Demons let rise to shining heights only those who have gained knowledge of their own "shadow" and learned to overcome it.

Demons are by far more active and aggressive than most other entities, which makes an association with them more dangerous. They are easier to call and quicker to serve. It is extremely dangerous to enter into a pact that makes you dependent on one of these creatures. A demon can, for instance, confer riches, power, or eternal youth, provided that the recipient, after his demise, enters his sphere and serves him. Such a deal will always be very detrimental to the individual's further development.

Also beware of Satanic cults, which are often an adulteration of old customs. It is best to use the middle road and treat demonic beings with respect. They become really dangerous only when you fight them or try to master them by force.

Demons live in different areas and spheres of the planets, mostly in ranks constructed a lot like human ones. They, too, have kings, princes, employees, and messengers. The demons of the Mars- and the Sun-spheres are the most dangerous. The invocation of such an entity can physically and psychologically kill the one who summons it immediately. In general, a demon should be invoked only by someone who possesses good self-awareness and ample clarity.

A few of the best known "rulers of darkness" are the archetypal demons Ashmodai and his wife Lilith, Beelzebub, Leviathan, Astaroth, Asmodeus, and Balbireth. (I include in this category the Petra-Loa or Haitian demons.) They work with the dark depths of the unconscious. In addition, there are a number of sex-demons who join individuals with unrealized desires. Their preferred abodes are often cloisters. The male sex-demon is called an incubus, the female, a succubus.

An experienced magician is able to employ these demons successfully for the fulfillment of desires via sex-magical practices. But extreme caution is warranted in any association with these creatures, since succubi can energetically suck their human partner dry if he loses control over them. This is not a factor for female magicians in an association with male sex-demons, but in these cases, there is a risk of sexual dependency.

Self-Created Demons

This is about ghouls, shadows, or phantoms. Ghouls are usually created unconsciously by strong emotional agitation. They become stronger as the agitated condition repeats itself. By their very presence they in turn create the urge to experience this sensation anew, since they are nourished by these energies.

With shadows, the situation is similar. In contrast to ghouls, they are created by a conscious act, a wishful imagination. They can solidify themselves by repetition, so that eventually, they are able to make themselves physically noticeable. They are also a cause of mass hysteria.

Phantoms are ghostly apparitions that take the place of the deceased. They are created by a transfigured memory of the living, and they often pretend to be the ghost of the deceased person. Most of the apparitions that appear at seances, as well as trickster ghosts and poltergeists belong to this group. Ancestor worship in many cultures, as in the Voodoo cult, has its origin in the unconscious creation of phantoms. These creatures are often unpredictable and even harder to dispel than a genuine demon.

Werewolves

Reports of people, who at night, especially at the full moon, are transformed into wolves, have been found in many cultures from time immemorial. A werewolf is not to be confused with a human who believes himself to be a wolf. Traditionally, in his human appearance, the werewolf is supposed to be recognizable as a wolf by his bushy eyebrows that meet in the middle and overly long middle fingers. After his transformation into a wolf, he still has human eyes and a human voice. Other comparable transformations into animals are known from other continents—the hyena-men from Africa, for instance, and the berserker from Scandinavia, a kind of werebear.

Numerous reports seem to confirm that such creatures do indeed exist. Opinions differ only about their looks—is it really a physical transformation or the transference of an energy-body in the shape of a wolf? Men suspected of being werewolves have often been injured while in their wolf's shape. When they were afterwards found in their homes, they exhibited on their human form the wounds inflicted on the wolf. However, reports about a transformation of a human being into a wolf and vice versa in front of witnesses are rare. This speaks for astral projection (the transmission of an energetic body), which can be fully active on the material level.

Only those with displaced malicious or sadistic inclinations will change into werewolves. This happens during the night, when the energetic body separates from the physical body. Then, other lowly beings, who feel attracted by the negative oscillations, can take possession. Under their influence, the energetic body attains a denseness that makes action on the material level possible. This occupation during sleep explains the human wolves' initial ignorance. They often realize only after a considerable period of time that they go through a transformation on certain nights. The change will gradually affect their material appearance. Wolf-like behavior will also show up in their daily life—for instance, in a kind of frenzy. It is said to have happened that a man finally became a wolf entirely.

It is a peculiarity of the Voodoo cult that it believes that only women change into werewolves. In Africa and Haiti, in rural communities, the women who are affected by this curse are generally known. They are not bothered, and the interaction with them is not different from other people. In the Voodoo cult, many are convinced that such a woman is burdened with serious guilt either from her present or an earlier life, and that she must now suffer for it in this form. The idea of a karmic family fate affecting several generations often plays a role too: the curse is passed on to the female heirs.

In Haiti, it is believed that another cause can lead to a woman's becoming a werewolf. She made, probably unconsciously, a pact with a demon. Perhaps the woman had ordered a murder from a sorcerer, and the sorcerer had promised a human sacrifice to the demon who would carry it out. If the woman would not abide by those conditions, the demon might make her into a wolf so that she would have to hunt humans on whose vital energies and sufferings he could nourish himself. Most demons are insatiable by nature. Therefore, they will make sure that the woman turns into a wolf again and again, providing sustenance for them. Werewolves are thus perpetrators and victims at the same time.

Female werewolves are usually keen on children. Like vampires, however, werewolves must first obtain the victim's permission or that of its parents. They try to talk unsuspecting mothers into letting them take away the child, or they get the mother's consent while she is dozing. Whichever way it happens, the permission can never be withdrawn. The best protection is knowledge, a heightened awareness, and attention.

In Haiti, another protective measure is taken in order to save newborns from attack. Werewolves detest bitter blood. In order to change the quality of the child's blood, a pregnant woman is given bitter black coffee mixed with cheap spirits and three drops of oil. In addition, the woman takes herbal butter with garlic, thyme, onions, manioc (or cassava), nutmeg, and other local herbs. Right after birth, the child is bathed in a brew of the same ingredients and then held over a flame of burning spirits (without burning it, of course). Thereafter, the child is given herbal teas to keep its blood bitter. During the ritual, the mother must confirm loudly three times that she and she alone is claiming possession of the child.

Werewolves are vulnerable to ordinary weapons made out of iron and steel. What makes them so dangerous is their combination of human intellect and animal strength.

Djinns

The term *djinn* comes from the Arabic and stands for a certain kind of elemental being. In some cultures, djinns are assigned to the element of air, since they can move through the air with very great speed. European wizards, however, assign them to the family of fire spirits, which corresponds to their appearance (see the sketch on page 112) and, as with all elemental spirits, is consistent with their attitudes. Therefore, they are summoned with the invocation for fire spirits (see page 122), who are subject to their ruler Azazael. Among the djinns are, on the one hand, quite well-meaning characters, and on the other, very evil-minded ones. Yet even the most friendly among them are always ready for a prank.

The djinns lead a really dissolute life and in the course of time have mingled with many races. Their chimera-like form (Chimeras are monsters with a lion-like upper body and goat horns, while their lower bodies are serpent-like and scaly.) derives from this intermingling, and from all the participants caught in it. There are reports about marriages between djinns and men, in which the djinn took on human form. There were also children from these marriages. They all possessed magic powers.

It is said that djinns can exert great power over humans, especially during sleep. There, they seem to influence the dreams and astral travel (the moving of the energetic body). Such a creature can also materially take people or things with the speed of the wind to any location. At times, a magician can make friends with a djinn and gain his support for the fulfillment of wishes, but it must be clear to the magician from the beginning that he has to reciprocate. A wise man acknowledges this right at the start, so that a pact is made between the djinn and the magician.

Vampires

Stories about vampires who at night suck out human or animal blood or vital energies come from all over the world. There are three different forms of manifestations in this category: First is the classic vampire, who sucks the vital energies out of the body of the living being—human or animal—in the form of blood. Second is the bodyless demon, who robs his victims of vital powers in their energetic form. And third type are humans who draw off the energy of another human in order to strengthen themselves with it.

Classic Vampires

The best-known vampire is Dracula, a character from a novel by Bram Stoker, who took as his model the historical Rumanian Count Vlad V., called Vlad Dracul. He brutally mistreated his subjects and prisoners. It has been said that this archetypal form of the vampire would suck other people's blood at night, and that he possessed the ability to change into a wolf, a bat, or even into heavy fog. Similar figures appear in other cultures, as, for instance, the lion-men of Africa. All these forms have in common the fangs and the cadaverous odor that makes them recognizable.

Embodied vampires, however, are rather rare. There is the report of a young man in a hospital who was observed drinking blood donations by the liter (vampires, too, keep pace with the times). When he was about to be trapped, he jumped out of a sixth-floor window and ran off without any injuries. Stories are also told about a mixed form of vampire—humans who leave their bodies during the night and fly to their victims to devour their vital energies.

Significantly more numerous are bodyless demons who move mainly on the energetic level and rob their victims of life-energies. They are often seduction-demons that the victim has consciously or unconsciously summoned. Such beings are attracted by strong displaced desires: they can be found, for instance, in cloisters. The succubus, the female seduction-demon, is the more common. She can gradually weaken her male partner so much that he falls ill and finally dies. The incubus, the male seduction-demon, however, is not so dangerous to his female partner. He rather causes in her a pathologically high sexual drive. Similar demons can also be self-created by vivid sexual fantasizing—these are phantoms. If they are successful in gaining power over their human partners, they can also confer a life-threatening consumption.

Vampire Demons

Beyond that, there are more vampire-like living spirits who attack humans from within their own weaknesses. Here, too, the rule of analogy pertains: Like attracts like: weak, timid humans and those who have a propensity for depression are attacked by them. The spirits are in a difficult position: Often they are deceased entities who are caught in an intermediate realm and have not found the way into the hereafter. They feel attracted by low oscillations of sadness and fear and feed on them. That, in turn, aggravates the victim's condition—the clinics are full of such cases. Here, it is important to recognize in time what is happening. Possession by a vampire is recognizable by its outer characteristics: movements are uncontrolled, slow, and halting; the skin has little elasticity and a parchment-like look or gelatin-like feel; the glance is veiled and empty. The victim also often injures himself slightly and, losing small amounts of blood, becomes weaker and weaker. One of the insidious qualities of vampires is their habit of appearing very fond (seduction-demons) of children. This deception, however, is detectable.

There are various ways to get rid of a vampire:

If a vampire was willing or unknowingly called by the use of magic symbols or vèvès, destroying those devices will prevent his further access and exile him.

If a vampire was invited by his victim, the exorcism is more involved. The invitation may not always have been uttered consciously. If the victim's level of sadness, fear, and depression are low enough that they are to the vampire's liking, that alone is enough of an invitation. Exclamations such as "I wish I was dead," or "If only someone would release me from my suffering," are offers that these creatures will not refuse. Final agreement may take place on the dream level.

If the victim is strong enough, he can try to reclaim power over his own body. To do so, he begins with the part of his body that he still controls. He then expands this sense of mastery and returning strength so that it extends over his whole body. To that end, he may mentally call on spiritual helpers—either godly entities, patron spirits, or living people with a strong radiance. It is better yet for the person to be supported by family members and friends.

Next, the vampire must be chased out of the victim's surroundings. Since these creatures have a pronounced aversion toward all cleansing substances, the victim should take a bath in strong salt or seawater, while his neck, head, and hands are in addition rubbed with salt. Then, the whole house should be fumigated with incense (see the chapters on "Magic Aids" and "Protective Rituals"). For inner purification, the person needs to drink sage tea and eat a lot of garlic. It's advised that for a while he eat no meat. It is also important to lift his mood so that the vampire is no longer attracted to him. Do all the rituals that renew self-esteem and transmit courage and strength (see the chapter "Working Magic"). A vacation can also positively affect his radiance.

If these measures are not sufficient, or if the person is already too weak to help himself, it is vital for him to get advice from a local spirit-healer or an experienced sorcerer.

Human Energy Vampires

This third form of vampire is the normal human who makes it a habit to drain the energy out of their fellow humans. This kind of vampirism is comparatively widespread. A weakening by such a person is not evident at first, and if you are not constantly in the vampire's presence, you will recuperate soon. But living in the immediate surroundings of such a person becomes dangerous.

Typical of such an energy drain are words that arouse empathy and elicit support. Such a person maintains continually that he has had bad luck, has been hexed or cursed. He may describe his employer as a demon and his banker as a monster (which is why his bank account is so low). Since an energy vampire attracts people of similar character, he seeks as compensation a strong person whom he can tap regularly. This takes place when he gets this person's attention and complains to him in hours-long conversations.

The best way to detect a human energy vampire is through your own senses. If you feel weakened or not very well after you have met with certain people, then they may indeed be this form of vampire. The only help you can give is to bring this condition to their attention, so that a remedy can be found. Beyond that, it is better simply to stay away from them, since they are not likely to change their behavior.

Elementary Beings

Elementary beings are nature spirits that inhabit the elements. In no way are they to be mistaken for elementals, who are artificially created. They differ from human beings in that they are not made up of a combination of the four basic elements, but are of one element alone. In their attributes and temperament, they embody the element to which they belong.

Contrary to general opinion, elementary beings have an immortal soul, and the more highly developed of these spirits may be superior in many respects to humans or surpass them in all areas. In contacts with these elementary beings it is best to be friendly and amenable, without exerting any pressure or force. In rare cases, a low creature may become a nuisance by constantly playing tricks. In this case, a means of restraint may be used to chase it away.

Elementary beings also live, on their level, in a material world, a parallel dimension. The Celts categorized it as the "otherworld." These elementary beings enter our coarser world by a kind of astral journeying (see the chapter "Working Magic"), and can therefore be perceived only as ghostly creatures. The reverse happens when humans with their energy-body visit the otherworld. The elementary realms, however, do not have a material dimension as strong as our world.

On earth, elementary beings take on diverse tasks that serve the preservation of nature and life in general. No life could exist on our planet without their assistance. Many of these beings are well-inclined toward humans and willing to help in emergency situations. They also like to be included in magical works.

Water Creatures

The spirits of water guard and protect the oceans and all other waters on the planet. They preserve balance and harmony in these realms. Water creatures master all magnetic magical forms. They can bestow upon the magician the ability of water- and mirror-reading and provide knowledge of water magic. In this domain also belong fertility and immortality.

The spirits of the water are water nymphs, undines, mermaids, sirens, and water sprites. The water nymphs' outer appearance resembles the classic image of the mermaid. They mostly are very sensitive

and well-meaning beings who have rescued many a shipwrecked mariner from drowning. It may also happen that they pull a man whom they like down into the depths with them, without realizing that he cannot survive in their element. More dangerous are the sirens, who aim to bring mariners to ruin. In general, female water-spirits are quite active in this world and also very curious about men. Especially in earlier times, this has sometimes led to mixed marriages with human partners, whereby the water spirit had to leave her element.

In order to call water spirits, the first thing to do is to create a water atmosphere in which they can appear more easily. This is done by obstructing the flow of elements (see the chapter "Magic Exercises"). It is best to begin at a time in which the water-tattva is dominant (see the chapter "Magic Aids"). Another good time is at twilight. The room should be immersed in green light. Aiding the appearance are a water basin and the burning of incense consisting of myrrh and lotus or another water plant. Then, turn to the West and begin the invocation, which can be freestyle. Helpful support can be obtained by the water-viewing or magic mirror (see the chapter "Working Magic").

Well-known leaders of the male water spirits are Nicksa, Amasol, Ardiphne, Frmot, Laquotor, Gamholym, Wolgor, and Quothoi. Female water-spirits are Istiphul, Osipeh, Isaphil, and many more.

Fire Creatures

Creatures of fire include the Farisilles (male fire fairies), the Schallores (female fire fairies), and salamanders. Fire fairies are generally less aggressive than salamanders. To them falls mainly the task of limiting and checking a fire to a certain extent, while salamanders usually aim at spreading a fire. To do this, they follow lightning bolts down to the earth, immediately inciting flames. Male salamanders are generally much livelier than females. Marriages are rare among them and can be found only among highly developed representatives of this race. They fight with one another constantly.

Their favorite places are locations where a fire is smoldering, such as volcanoes, blast furnaces, in the hot gulf of the earth, and in the fireplaces of homes. Wherever a fire is lighted, even if it is only a candle, they are there right away. It is important to greet the salamander whenever a candle is lighted for magical purposes.

The form of the fire creature depends on its level of development. Low fire spirits especially have a strong urge to imitate. They often take on a chimera-like appearance (see page 112). Also typical for them is a reddish skin color, bristly hair, slanted eyes, and a small, triangular-shaped head. The traditional image of the Christian devil is to a large degree borrowed from the looks of the salamander.

Salamanders are capable of learning all kinds of magical manifestations that are based on the element of fire, and they can teach the magician a great deal about mastering its electrical powers. Fire is the basis of the destructive as well as the life-giving principle.

To invoke salamanders, you need to create a fiery atmosphere by damming the element (see the chapter "Magic Exercises"). The best times are during the fire-tattva (see the chapter "Magic Aids") or at noon. The light in the room should be red. Suitable as incense are frankincense, camphor, and especially the leaves of the stinging nettle. Lighting a fire or a candle also has a helpful effect. Then, take up a wand and face south for the invocation. Instead of the magic wand, you could use a trident, if you wish. Another way to contact salamanders is with a magic mirror (see the chapter "Working Magic").

Well-known rulers of the salamanders are: Michael (ruler of the sun and the lightning bolt), Samael (master of the volcanoes), Anael (prince of the astral light), also Pyrhum, Itumo, Focalor, Lakohem, Caymos, Ouohor, Tapheth, and Amtophul.

Air Creatures

To the airy element belong the sylphs, nature fairies, elves, and storm spirits. Creatures of the air often live together in lasting partnerships and like to carry out their work together.

Elves and nature fairies (devas) are responsible for protecting plants and providing them with vital energy. They bring about the blooming of flowers. They are shy in the face of humans. Other fairies and sylphs are more inclined to make contact with humans. Frequently, they assume the task of healing. Some of them know how to change misfortune into good fortune; others send out sudden intuitions. They govern the power of omniscience and the ability to read minds. As a result, they keep their distance from most humans, since false and deceitful thoughts are deeply abhorrent to them.

Air spirits exist in the higher realms of the air. They steer the air currents and winds. Especially highly developed air beings are often compared to angels or confused with them. The classic image of a delicate, winged angel really is the picture of a sylph. They sometimes let themselves grow wings for fun in order to appear in this manner.

All creatures of the air, with the exception of storm spirits, are delicate and slender. Elves vary in height from an inch or so to human size. Fairies, in contrast, can be much taller than humans. Their clothes are usually transparent and light like veils. They prefer lovely locations, such as beautiful gardens and parks, clearings, high mountain peaks, quiet forests, and sylvan glades.

Storm spirits are strikingly different. They are wild fellows with demon-like looks. Their misshaped, often bulky bodies are covered with black, coarse hair. They bring about storms and other violent happenings in nature and are similar to djinns.

Most magicians avoid close contact with creatures of the air,

since they are not often well-disposed to man and are, in addition, hard to direct. If a magician incurs their displeasure, they can quickly harm or even kill him. Only if you do not wish to control them, but just want a friendly relationship, should you risk invoking them.

At the beginning of an invocation, the air element must be strengthened in the room (see the chapter "Magic Exercises"). Choose the air tattva or the morning twilight. The lantern should emit a bluish or greenish light. The incense used can be of rosebuds, hazel bush buds, or violets. Face East, and with a feather (an eagle feather is best), draw the magic pentagram (see the chapter "Magic Symbols") in the air. This is followed by the calling of the fairies and elves.

The leading creatures of the air are: Paralda, Glisi, Cargoste, Parahim, Cornelia, Coratiel, Coachiel, Agares, Barbatos, Fligor, and Dalep.

Earth Creatures

To the realm of the earth belong the gnomes, gremlins, black elves, and hobgoblins. Unlike gnomes, black elves and hobgoblins are not really well-disposed toward humans. It is best, therefore, to stay away from them. The gnomes are usually friendly and well-meaning, as long as you don't invade and destroy their realm.

Earth spirits prefer dwelling in the mountains, in canyons, dense forests, and between the roots of gnarly, old trees. Some of them stay mainly in caves under the ground and inside mountains. There they protect the treasures of the earth and the crystals, whose growth they oversee and guide. Furthermore, they are responsible for the growth of plants, whom they provide with vital energy through the roots. They also act as guardian spirits to animals and children.

Gnomes are approximately 18 to 90 inches (1/2 to 2-1/2m) tall. They usually prefer to dress in a medieval style, consisting of a jacket, shirt, trousers, and peaked shoes. Their typical head gear is a peaked cap. They look very much like humans. The more a gnome evolves, the nicer his facial features are. The underdeveloped ones among them are sometimes deformed or have bestial limbs.

Gnomes who dwell on earth imitate humans: they celebrate the local festivals, marry, and live in a similar structure to that of people in their home area. A gnome couple typically stays together for life and is faithful to each other. On earth, however, it is mainly male gnomes who are active, while the women are hardly ever seen.

Gnomes have a particular passion for trade. They also expect you to reciprocate if they do you a favor or provide a service. The magician can learn much from them about herbs, healing remedies, and material apparitions.

To prepare for the invocation, the earth element in the room is dammed-up (see the chapter "Magic Exercises"). You should also wear white. The invocation should be begun during the earth tattvas or around midnight. Styrax and also thuja serve as incense. Yellow light is recommended. Offerings should consist of fruit (especially bananas), and nuts, placed on a white cloth. For the invocation, face North and draw a pentagram into the air.

Well-known gnome leaders are Gob, Mentifil, Andimo, Orova, Erami, Buriel, Salvian, Durin, Achimaei, Gaziel, Fegor, and Antologan.

Goblins

Goblins are small nature spirits who belong to the earth element. Among them are extremely vicious creatures and also extremely well-meaning ones. As is the case with all elementary spirits, their character traits are reflected in their appearance and physiognomy. While human standards cannot always be applied, it is certain that goblins with distorted and disproportional facial features do not have good intentions. The more evolved, the more harmonious is the creature's outer appearance. Their leaders sometimes have almost human features and can reach towering heights.

The goblins' favorite dwelling place is out in nature, especially in densely wooded areas and bushes. They often live in an almost symbiotic relationship with plants, which they nurture and protect, and from whose fruits and energies they in turn feed themselves. As a result, they often embody the attributes of the plants in whose environment they stay. Those who live surrounded by poisonous plants, for example, are not especially well-inclined toward humans. These little people can become extremely irate if their environment is destroyed. It is advisable to approach all plants in the forest with respect so as not to attract their anger.

In addition to the shy forest goblins, there are other groups who prefer to stay near human habitation or actually inside humans' houses. Hobgoblins belong to this group. Although they are mostly harmless, they are always ready to play a trick. If you discover that you have such a co-dweller, it is quite possible to make friends with him. You can do it by giving him small presents in the form of fruit, nuts, and glittering objects. Put them into a corner reserved especially for him. These little beings will thank you for your hospitality either with material goods or by warning you of dangers of all kinds—spiritual attacks, for example, or false friends.

If you want to invite a goblin into your house—one who will take pleasure in giving you gold and other riches—you need to carry out a certain ritual. This creature is the so-called Puck, a goblin who is especially bold and mischievous and wants to be continually employed. The best time to attract him is on New Year's night. Walk backwards seven times around the borders of seven fields, without turning around. When you have completed this task, Puck announces himself. At that point you need to ask him, "Who are you? What do you want? Would you like to help me? Then come with me!" If one day, you should want to get rid of this rather hyperactive creature, you need only give him a red jacket and say good-bye.

The sketch on page 129 shows a goblin from the species of the Twark, 10 to 12 inches (20 to 30cm) tall, as he once showed himself to me in the Dartmoor, near the Southern-English town of Tavistock.

Beings of the Ether

The dragon and the sphinx can be assigned to the intangible sphere of the ether. As an ether-being, the dragon can appear in all elementary realms, as fire serpent, for instance, or sea monster. It is an ambivalent creature that, on the one hand, can appear as guardian and protector, and on the other, destroy whole regions with ferocious force. Dragons are no longer directly active on the earth, but they are always present as a materialized primeval force.

The Druids (Celtic priests), who had a pronounced dragon cult, considered the earth itself as the body of the Great Dragon. The energy channels of the earth were therefore called dragon lines. Along these fields, megaliths were erected and stone circles built.

Dragons are very old creatures who possess great wisdom and a pronounced sense of justice. They have great imaginations and an abundance of ideas, which makes them desirable teachers. It makes sense to foster a connection with them, since they guard the ether, which is timeless and without dimension, especially if you are planning to traverse it. The ether can after all be traversed not only with energy—and spirit bodies—but also with the material body.

The following invocation of a dragon comes from the "Book of Pheeryllt." It customarily takes place in the open, at a high location, but it can also be carried out, in a slightly modified form, in a room.

Go at noon to a suitable location where you have formed a large, magic circle out of twelve stones. Draw the symbol of the dragon eye (see the sketch to the right) in the middle of the circle with the magic sword. Then, sprinkle some iron- or gold-dust on it. Next, dragon blood or dragon skin (see the chapter "Magic Aids") is smudged (smoked) within the circle.

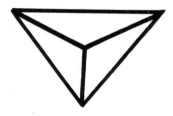

After that, step into the center of the dragon eye and hold the magic sword high above your head with its tip pointing to the ground. While in this posture, call out the invocation of the Dragon three times loudly and distinctly:

Cum saxum saxorum, in duersum montum oparum da —
in aetibulum, in quinatum: Draconist!

Then thrust the sword with a quick movement deep into the ground. Following this, sit in a meditative posture in the middle of the dragon eye and wait for the dragon to appear. In order to capture him, you must pull the sword out of its body. Only then is it safe to leave the protective circle.

Well-known dragons are the primeval Tiamat and the horrible Fafnyr.

Other Creatures of the Different Planet Spheres

In the region called the sphere of the earth, different entities live in shifting dimensions. This region is called the zone. The same pertains to the other planets in whose surroundings live other influential entities. The gods of many cultures—also the loa of Voodoo—come in part from the spheres of planets. The description of the Haitian gods (see the chapter "The Loa—Gods of Voodoo") lists some of the major deities.

The following characterizations of the various regions may be helpful for an invocation. The planets that are not mentioned have no special influence on the development of this earth, at least not yet. Interested persons can, of course, also make contact with these spheres. But for magic, they are of no significance. If you want to occupy yourself with sphere-magic, it is advisable to proceed in the order described so as to suffer no harm. This also holds true for journeys with the spirit- and energy-body in these spheres.

The Orbital Zone of the Earth

In the orbital zone of the earth there are 360 heads; each one rules over the earth for minutes in the course of a day. In addition, there are many more entities, such as elemental beings, demons, etc. To call them, you need to write the symbol or name of the entity on a round piece of paper. If you want to use an amulet to reach one of these entities, it should also be round. You need ten candles. The jinni of the earth zone can be helpful with this magic progression and perhaps also bestow the required abilities.

The Sphere of the Moon

The sphere of the moon is ruled by 28 positive and 29 negative jinni. There, too, are a number of other entities. They influence the electromagnetic power fields of the earth. In addition, they favorably influence sensitivity and ecstasy. You can learn the use of magnetic powers from them. In order to call them, place nine candles. Any amulets should be made out of silver. Their day is Monday.

The Sphere of Mercury

Mercury is under the influence of 72 Mercury-jinni. Their attributes correspond to the 72 tarot cards. The Mercury sphere influences all gaseous processes on earth. The spiritual body and all spiritual work are subject to it. For an invocation, place eight candles. Amulets should be made of brass and have an octagonal shape. The corresponding day is Wednesday.

The Sphere of Venus

Presiding over the sphere of Venus are 90 intellect-beings who influence love, attraction, and fertility. Contact with this sphere evokes a lovelorn condition that is not easy to control. For an invocation, place seven candles that generate a greenish light (for instance, storm lanterns with green glass). Amulets need to be of copper—a metal that is suitable for all love-charms—and should be in the shape of a heptagon (a heptagonal star, for example). The corresponding day is Friday.

The Sphere of the Sun

Governed by 45 jinni, the sun sphere influences the vital energy of the earth and all physical processes. The spiritual, energetic, and physical body are held together by its energy. For an inexperienced magician it can be dangerous to establish contact with this sphere: an intolerance to the oscillations can arise and cause considerable damage. For the invocation, place six candles that give a yellow light. Sun amulets can be made from gold. The corresponding day is Sunday.

The Sphere of Mars

There are 36 known rulers of this sphere. They release in man and animal the instinct of self-preservation. Striving for power, conducting war, physical strength, passion, and eroticism belong to their radius of action. The negative entities promote murder and death and other means of destruction. All entities of this sphere are extremely dangerous, even the most positive ones and should never be called by an inexperienced magician. To this group also belong some members of the Haitian Petro-Loa. For their invocation, five candles are placed that emit a red light. Mars amulets should be made out of iron and have a pentagonal shape. Tuesday corresponds with this sphere.

The Sphere of Jupiter

The sphere of Jupiter is governed primarily by the 12 original jinni that have contact with the signs of the zodiac. Their sphere of influence embraces the entire cosmic world order. These entities lead evolution's path to perfection. They influence and strengthen man's sense of justice. For their invocation, four candles are placed that emit a blue light. A Jupiter symbol should be square and made of tin. The corresponding day is Thursday.

The Sphere of Saturn

This sphere is governed by 49 jinni who rule over the fate of the mineral, plant, and animal world. The sphere of Saturn influences man's intuition and conscience. This so-called karmic sphere is associated with the ether. Saturn entities oversee the activities of all beings and allow to a certain degree the most deplorable actions and demonic activities—all within karmic strictures. They monitor the fulfillment of the fate of all beings. The sphere of Saturn is harder to reach than any of the other spheres. Only a very experienced magician can dare to call beings of this region, since its vibrations can hardly be borne. It can lead not only to a physical death, but also to an energetic one. For the invocation, three candles are placed that emit a violet light. The corresponding shape is a triangle and the metal is lead. The day governed by Saturn is Saturday.

5.
Magic Symbols

The Circle

The magic circle is the most important of all magic symbols. It stands for infinity, which is without beginning and without end. All rituals and all magical action take place within the circle. When the magician is in the circle, he embodies the microcosm within the macrocosm, conducting his magic according to the hermetic principle "as above, so below." When inside the circle, the magician represents the divine power of creation. If the circle was drawn correctly, he is safe there from the reach of other entities.

The magic circle is drawn in different ways depending on the cultural region. The work is interwoven with the regional god-image. Invocation formulas are suitable only for a certain cultural circle; elsewhere they have no effect. It is most appropriate for the magician to develop his own formula with which to express his intention. As is the case with all magic procedures, it is also important for the drawing of the circle that the magician totally concentrate on the power of his will.

If the circle is drawn outdoors, the ritual knife or sword is used. Indoors, you can draw with chalk, while scattering pulverized herbs. A circle of oil—an ethereal oil such as oil of rosemary—also affords effective protection: just spread it evenly in a circle. Especially practical is a circle that is embroidered or painted on a piece of fabric. The cloth can be spread out at the beginning of the ritual without any further preparation.

The size of the circle depends on the kind of ritual and the available space. Make sure that there is sufficient space to stay in it comfortably and move around.

The Triangle

The magic triangle is a symbol of revelation. It is a diagram of the three realms that a thought must penetrate for its realization—spirit, energy, and body. On the spiritual level, its three aspects signify will, intellect, and feeling. On the energetic level, they belong to power, order, and life. In the material world, the uppermost peak represents neutral causal energy, which divides towards the bottom into an electrical charge and a magnetic one, then assuming material form in the horizontal basic line.

The number three plays a key role in many cultures and religions (think of the trinity in Christian belief, which had its origin in the three forms of appearance of the primordial goddess—virgin, mother, crone). If the three is multiplied by itself, the result is nine, the number of perfection. The three is associated with karma, and is therefore a fateful number, belonging to Saturn.

If you are calling a spirit entity, draw the triangle outside the magic circle. Outdoors, you can draw it with a sword (see the chapter "Magic Aids") or a knife. Indoors, draw the triangle with chalk on the ground or on paper. You can also create a special piece of fabric with the symbol on it. The triangle must be large enough so that the entity called can comfortably fit into it. When you call a spirit into a triangle, it can leave only after you send it off. Higher entities especially need this aid in order to appear in the material world.

While drawing the triangle, you must have the highest level of concentration, imagining that reality is created out of the will, according to the divine principle. In the center of the triangle, put a symbol or portrayal of the entity with whom you want to establish contact. Other means can also assist the appearance of the entity: a bowl of water for a mermaid, appropriate incense for a fire spirit, or potting earth for a goblin—there are no limits to the possibilities.

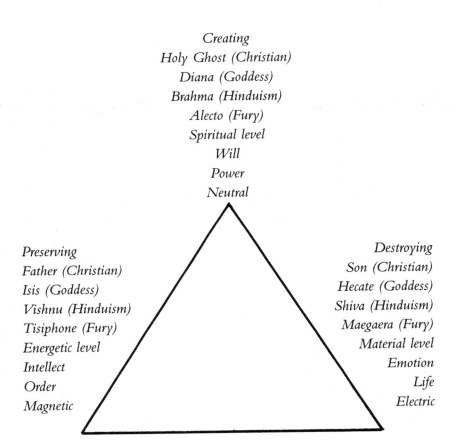

Creating
Holy Ghost (Christian)
Diana (Goddess)
Brahma (Hinduism)
Alecto (Fury)
Spiritual level
Will
Power
Neutral

Preserving
Father (Christian)
Isis (Goddess)
Vishnu (Hinduism)
Tisiphone (Fury)
Energetic level
Intellect
Order
Magnetic

Destroying
Son (Christian)
Hecate (Goddess)
Shiva (Hinduism)
Maegaera (Fury)
Material level
Emotion
Life
Electric

The Pentagram

The pentagram is also called the pentacle or the Druid's foot. It is a five-pointed star, drawn in one line, and a very old symbol of power that signifies control over the elements. Its form is that of a man with outstretched arms and legs (there is a very well-known drawing of this by Leonardo da Vinci). The lower four points stand for the tangible elements of fire, water, earth, and air. The upper point, denoting the head, symbolizes the spirit and thus the element of ether, the akasha principle.

Many magicians use the pentacle to force spirit entities under their control and to instill reverence in them. Generally, it is very useful in the invocation of elementary entities (see the chapter "Demons, Elementary Spirits, Entities of the Spheres"). Moreover, it provides effective protection against negative energies and spiritual attacks by hostile entities. That's why it is recommended that this symbol be applied to magical robes. If worn as an amulet, it aids in personal undertakings and strengthens your power over your own development.

In calling spirit entities, pull the pentagram down from the peak toward the left, from there up to the right, across to the outer left, then to the right below and from there again upward, but leave it so that the peak remains slightly open (see the upper sketch). You can draw it on the ground or on a piece of paper, or in the air with the magic wand (see the chapter "Magic Aids"), while you imagine the lines as glowing bands of light.

At the end of the ritual, after you dismiss the spirit entities, close the pentagram from the bottom up. Begin on the left bottom side and pull the line up to the top, from there to the right below, to the outer left, across to the right outside, and again to the left below (sketch on the bottom). Note that, the point on the left bottom remains slightly open. Unwanted beings and energies can be banned using this shape.

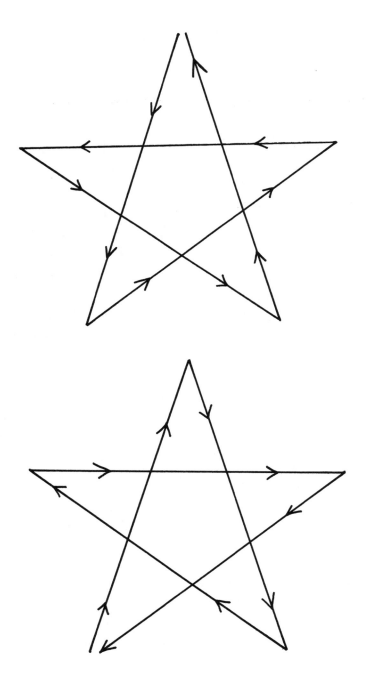

The Spiral

The Right-Rotating Spiral

The right-rotating spiral relates to all that is to happen on earth (climbing plants, for instance, grow clockwise). If you have a wish or want to affect a magic occurrence in our world, you can do it using a right-rotating spiral. Draw it on a large sheet that you place under the ritual altar. You can also add the spiral symbol to other aspects of your magic to make it more powerful.

If you have a good imagination, you can avail yourself of a very powerful technique. First, imagine the desired object before your eyes. Concentrate on this picture for a few minutes. Then surround it in your mind, clockwise, from top to bottom, with a shining white spiral. You can also carry out the movement with a magic wand.

Another method is meditation. Draw the spiral on a piece of paper, initiating the alpha state, a trance-like condition such as the one you get into before falling asleep. After a while, steer your desire into the spiral, either in a visual image or clad in words. This can concern material wishes or the attainment of special abilities.

Rejuvenation

With the spiral, you can carry out a special meditation that creates physical and spiritual rejuvenation. The right-rotating spiral corresponds to the cell spirals in the body, the DNA. In the course of life, the number of rotations increases; that means the spiral rotates from the outside more and more towards the center, which finally leads to stagnation and death. Understanding this secret is the key to the physical rejuvenation that, of course, always accompanies a spiritual rejuvenation.

Draw a large sketch of a right-rotating spiral on a piece of paper. Keep your eyes fixed on the drawing for some time while breathing deeply. Then let your eyes grasp the innermost point in the middle of the spiral and follow the line from the inside out, until you feel that you have achieved the highest energy level possible for you. Repeat the exercise several times until a powerful movement arises. Use your imagination to guide this movement into your body. Finally, give an order to all cells to open up the spiral to the desired point in a right-rotating direction. You can relay this order to the unconscious by words, or visualize the cells. With serious daily repetition, physical rejuvenation will soon take place.

The Left-Rotating Spiral

The left-rotating spiral has an effect that is opposite to the right-rotation. It generates a whirl that leads out of the earthly plateau, affecting the dispersion of energies. This example impressively illustrates the power of the left-rotation: The walls of Jericho, believed to be indestructible, simply collapsed after attackers marched day and night in uniform steps to the left around the town. This created a stagnant wave with a destructive effect.

For magic purposes, you can use the left-rotating spiral to disperse undesirable energies. To achieve this effect, just think the undesirable situation into the spiral. Focused imagination is decisive for success.

The left-rotating spiral is very effective in the treatment of illnesses. With the aid of a spiritually generated whirl, illnesses can be drawn out of the body and dissolved. Put the spiral directly on the focal point of the illness and remove it from the body by left-rotation. If the whole organism is affected, mentally wrap the patient, starting from the feet, in a spiral of white light. After reaching the head, the spiral will lead on into the ether and dissolve. Then you can begin with the patient's energetic restoration.

You can also use the left-rotating spiral for purposes of defense. If you are dealing with an opponent who seems physically superior to you, visualize a living image of the opponent and wrap him up before your inner eye with a left-rotating, shining ribbon, starting at the head and working down to the feet. Visualize vividly the person's power disappearing into the void. In most cases, your opponent will become aware of the loss of power and forgo an attack.

As with all magical work, the power of your will and imagination is decisive here. Practice makes perfect.

The Double Spiral

The double spiral is a symbol of the alternating effects of the physical and the energetic worlds. It represents the nexus of the dimensions.

In meditation, it can serve as an aid to the spirit or energetic body in visiting other worlds (see the chapter "Magic Exercises"). This procedure comes from an old Celtic tradition for getting to the otherworld: Sit down in a comfortable position and place a piece of paper in front of you with the picture of the double spiral on it. Devote your full attention to it for a few minutes, and then close your eyes and focus inwardly on the starting point in the center of the right-rotating spiral. Now, consciously transport yourself to this point and begin following the spiral to the right, step-by-step. After making some turns, you will reach a point at which the energy changes. On the energetic level, this point is customarily protected by two guards who will not let every traveler pass. If entrance is denied, you must turn back immediately.

If passage is granted, follow the left-rotating spiral into the center. The area surrounding the center point is at first clad in thick swathes of fog that only lighten after you reach the center point. There, a completely different world opens up. The term "other-world" does not denote a specific place, but is rather a collective term for all reachable parallel dimensions that exist in our world in different time and vibration levels. If you meet other beings in this place, approach them with respect. If orders or prohibitions are issued, follow them without exception.

In order to end the visit to the otherworld, return via the same route that took you there. Again start in the center of the left-rotating spiral and follow its windings out clockwise. At the turning point between the two spirals, turn left to enter the counterclockwise spiral. When you reach the center and your consciousness is again in the here and now, you can conclude the meditation. Open your eyes and stretch in order to feel your body again.

The Triple Whirl

The triple whirl (triskelion or triskele) is a universal symbol that was much in favor with the Celts. Like the triangle, it represents the three levels: the spiritual, the energetic, and the material. The spirals have a transmitting effect: every cause on one level releases on another level. Thus,

it is a symbol of magical workings, illustrating the energetic links. As an aid to meditation, the triple whirl can be helpful in the comprehension of magic connections. In the form of an amulet, it strengthens the will and can bring about changes on all levels.

Vèvès

In Haiti, unlike other cults that use statues and pictures—drawings are made that symbolize the gods invoked. They can be drawn on the ground with corn flour, brick dust, bark, or coffee grounds. These pictures are called vèvès. The priest draws the vèvè in fine lines on the ground during the ritual by letting the powder drift between forefinger and thumb down to the ground. While he does this, he is accompanied by the followers' traditional songs that are designed to lift the energy of the room to the desired level.

The symbols of the vèvè embody the gods, the Loa, and bring them into contact with the conjurer. In the Haitian Voodoo cult, this divine manifestation appears like a form of madness. The entity manifests itself in one of the people present, who involuntarily uses its characteristic gestures, abilities, and facial expressions for the duration of the ceremony. Moving in a kind of trance, the possessed person regains control of his body only after the ritual has ended.

When the priest has finished the drawing, he sprinkles it with offerings in the form of grilled maize and other dried food. He pours a mild liquor on the drawing as a sacrificial offering. After repeating this three times, he swings his rattle above the drawing and speaks his ritual formula. Then, he puts a candle on the vèvè. At this point, the other dignitaries of the cult extend greetings to the Loa by pouring water on the picture. The corpses of sacrificial animals are also placed on it. Particular objects and plants that belong to the

Loa are also placed on the vèvè.

These drawings originated in Africa, and their style is unique. Here is a vèvè that serves for the invocation of several gods. In the original, it covered an area of six times six meters (almost 120 feet).

1) Symbol of ritual drums
2) Symbol of Agwe-Taroyo
3) Symbol of Ogu-Badagri
4) Magic symbol for collecting energy
5) Symbol of the goddess Erzulie
6) Symbol of the god Damballah-Wédo
7) Symbol of other ritual drums

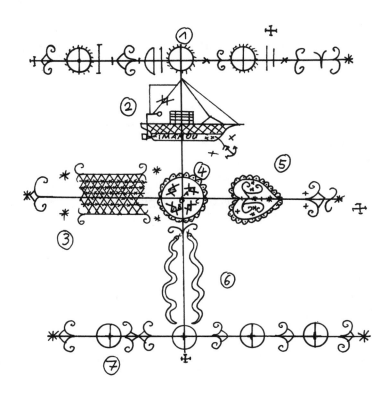

Correct Use of the Vèvè

In order to create a vèvè for a large ceremony, the hungan (voodoo priest) must have extensive knowledge and years of experience. It is a complicated science, whose details can only be learned from a Haitian hungan in an initiation. Many-faceted invocation pictures, such as the one on page 149 are used only at very lavish group ceremonies. Extreme caution is recommended when you are working with this vèvè. This warning holds true for the use of all the vèvès, especially those of demon entities who deal in harmful magic. Some of the especially dangerous Loa have the habit of requesting offerings again and again long after they have been provided.

A magician can easily become dependent on a demon. An entity may even regard an inexperienced magician himself as a sacrificial offering and seriously harm him. The vèvès of the demons are shown only to demonstrate the practices of bokors (black magic practitioners), so that unsuspecting persons can detect harmful sorcery and deflect it. If there is a reasonable suspicion that an individual has been cursed, and he finds a note or an object with the vèvè of such an entity, appropriate countermeasures should be undertaken right away (see the chapter "Protecting Rituals").

For magic, the gods' vèvès are to be used according to their attributes. Starting point is always the vèvè of Legba, since he opens the way to the realm of the spirits. The vèvè of the appropriate Loa is added. The power of love magic can be enhanced by adding to the objects used (candles, amulets, herb bags) the vèvès of Legba and Erzulie.

If a magic object is to be charged with a god's power, the appropriate vèvè is drawn with chalk or corn flour on the floor next to the one of Legba. Then the object, together with some sacrificial offerings, is placed in the center. The offerings correspond to the favorites of the entities you are calling. The moderate Petra-Loa, as well as most of the members of the Gédé-family, are satisfied with an egg and a lot of rum instead of a blood sacrifice. Demons adjust themselves to the customs of the country, so that instead of the ritual butchering of an animal, a sausage might be offered. Eggs especially entice spirit entities, for they carry in them the energy of germinating life that has no will.

After the place of ritual has been prepared with the vèvès, the invocation of the god begins. Candles are placed and lighted in the colors and quantities appropriate to the god. Suitable incense is also used at times. Then, the priest sits down on the ground at the lower end of the vèvè. In his right hand, he holds a magic wand or magic pointer. If demons are to be called, he additionally armors himself with a magic sword or dagger that he carries in his belt. A thick circle of salt is also drawn around the vèvè so that entities cannot cross the line.

At the beginning of the invocation, the priest thanks Legba for opening the door and begs him for protection and strength. Then he loudly calls the name of the god whom he wants to invoke and presents his concerns. The Loa is asked to enter into the object and charge it with his power. During the invocation, the priest steadfastly keeps his magic wand pointed at the object in the middle of the vèvè as a road sign, so to speak, for the Loa. After the incantation, the priest enters a trance-like state and waits attentively for a sign that announces the arrival of the god, who most often shows himself through a strong vibration of the wand, and sometimes also by sudden changes of room temperature or ground vibrations. It is not unusual for some Loa of the Petro group to experience strong feelings of constriction, and animals and even insects become silent suddenly.

When the priest is certain that the Loa has arrived, he repeats, if possible, his invocation seven times and begs for active support for his undertaking. If the vibrations of the wand have calmed down, he can assume that the Loa has entered the object with his energy and is agreeable to the offering. The object, so blessed by the Loa, is a highly effective tool and can be used after the end of the ritual for its agreed upon purpose.

After an appropriate span of time—in traditional Haitian Voodoo ceremonies can stretch over several hours or even days—the Loa are dismissed with a sentence that is repeated seven times:

I thank you, Loa, for your services
And let you go. Be blessed.

Thereafter, the vèvè is destroyed and the sacrificial offerings removed. If an egg has been offered, it is first broken on a plate so the Loa can be let go. The offerings left behind seem to be untouched, but the Loa have drawn from them all their fine-material energies in order to nourish themselves. Note: sacrificial fruits especially rot rapidly. The remains are therefore buried or thrown into flowing water.

If during the ritual Petro-Loa have been invoked, further protective measures are taken after their dismissal. The salt circle that encloses the vèvè remains overnight. In addition, incense is burned in the room for its repelling effect. The priest then takes a ritual bath with purifying substances. Sometimes he will even spend the following night in a specially drawn salt circle. This is certainly needed if he can still feel the demons' presence in the room.

Many of the Haitian Loa seem to be the equivalent of European and Asian gods. Damballah corresponds to the fire snake or the dragon of the Celtic religion. Hecate, the ancient witch goddess with destructive powers, has her counterpart in the Indian goddess Kali and in her Haitian embodiment Hekua Oya (Oya's original name in Sudanese). The god of the oceans, Agwe, equates to the ancient Greek Poseidon and Roman Neptune, and the beautiful Erzulie is the Aphrodite (Roman Venus) of the Voodoo cult. In the course of time, other religions, too, have taken over and adopted many of the Haitan or African gods. Even Christianity has received older gods into its circle of saints, as, for instance, Brigid, who was once revered as a goddess of light by the Celts.

Thus, the Loa are universal ancient powers and archetypes who are known by different names all over the world. In the practice of magic, therefore, the sorcerer chooses the form and kind of invocation that he relates to most, and that is most easily understood.

The Loa can be grouped into different combinations according to their goals and aims. They can strengthen a ritual very powerfully. That is because Voodoo has been practiced so actively up to the present time. Through being worshiped, the energy of the spirit entities increases, and they accumulate enough power to appear and become active in the material world. The vévé serves as the gate through which the Loa enters and leaves the world.

The Voodoo Pentacle

The Voodoo pentacle is a magic power symbol whose meaning is similar to that of the pentagram. A symbol of energy that radiates from its point of origin onto all levels, it is said to signify the rule over all areas of life. As a universal vévé, it adorns many implements used in Voodoo ceremonies. Through it, magically charged objects increase their effectiveness. It embodies the magician's power and during magical practices it is worn as an amulet around his neck, engraved in a round metal plate.

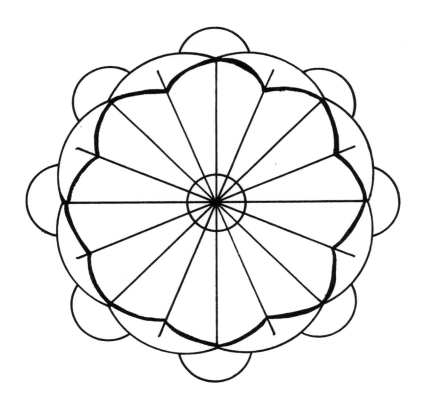

6.
Magic Aids

Clothing

The Garment

It is up to each magician to determine how lavish her ritual garment should be. Its main purpose is to protect her as much as possible from foreign influences from the spiritual and energetic worlds. When sending out spiritual or other energy, her body within remains safe from hostile entities.

Silk is the best material to use due to its insulating qualities. It is important for the garment to cover the entire body, with the exception of the hands, feet, and head. An attached hood may replace a hat in certain cases.

In the drawing on page 156, a Tibetan monk, disguised as a demon, is cleaning a place to prepare it for a ceremony. By wearing a mask and robe that correspond to a specific entity, the monk embodies its spirit and can make use of its powers. This particular costume is worn solely for the banishing of evil spirits. Garments dedicated to a special entity are suitable only for special rituals.

Modern magical garments are mostly simple cowls with a hood (see the sketch at the left), preferably made out of silk. The hood is not necessary, but it is practical. The cowl is held together by a magic cord or a magic belt.

Native Americans often made their ritual garments out of leather (sketch above), similar to the dance-garment of a shaman from the tribe of the Haida. It connected them during the ceremony with the spirits of different animals. Ritual paintings illustrated parts of the bear in a motif of the subarctic tribes. Stag hooves and beaks of birds were attached to the fringes. When the shaman moved, they made a rattling noise that was supposed to call forth the spirits. Fringes—whether out of leather or bark—have been very common in shamanic circles worldwide, since they dispel negative energies and evil spirits.

If you want to wear a magical garment, it is best to make it yourself or have it made according to your requirements. The color of the silk depends on the kind of magic you are practicing. You can, of course, obtain several garments, each one in a different color, to suit the level with which you're working (for corresponding colors, see the chapter "Working Magic"). Light violet, a universal color, corresponds in its vibrations to the all-embracing fifth element of ether. With a garment in this color, you can establish a connection with entities on all levels. For contact with especially powerful demons, black offers the best protection. White is used only with high entities of light and also with the gnomes. You can embroider the garment with symbols or embellish it in other ways.

When the garment is finished, you need to cleanse it from foreign energies under running water and iron it yourself. After that, make sure that the garment is not touched by anyone except yourself, and consecrate it by promising to wear it only for magic work.

The Hat

A magic hat can also be a cap, a band, or a metallic hoop. Silk and metal are especially recommended, since these materials insulate well. A head covering is useful for protecting your spirit from the influence of foreign thoughts and to strengthen your concentration. It also gets in the way of pesky spirit entities who want to achieve a possession. The magic head cover may be worn only for rituals. The making and the design of it are up to you, as are the magic symbols you embroider on it or engrave into it.

The Belt

According to the rules of ceremonial magic, the belt should be the same color as the robe, and preferably of silk or leather that comes from a powerful animal. Some spirits, however, are repelled by leather.

Like the garment, the belt should be made by you yourself. You can also adorn it with magical symbols of your choice—for instance, the pentagram (the Druid's foot, made from a five-pointed star drawn in one line, see page 143), a circle, a Star of David (two triangles that lie over each other so as to form a six-pointed star), runes (see the chapter "Working Magic"), or astrological symbols. The belt, too, should be worn only for magic rituals; at other times it needs to be carefully and safely stored together with the garment.

Witches of the Wicca tradition (based on the books of Gerald Brousseau Gardner, 1884–1964) wear a cord around the waist instead of a belt. It is made from thick, red yarn that has been twined into a long braid and is repeatedly slung around the waist. It is also used as a measurement for the magic circle.

Ritual Knives

Wooden Knives

Witches' knives made out of wood, such as the one shown at the left, are carved by their owners out of one piece, and, like the magic wand (page 164) are suitable for non-violent rituals. With a wooden knife, you can draw the magic circle or signs on the ground or into the air. In addition, you can use it to aim collected energies at a target. Moreover, you can give more power to a magic act by using the knife to etch letters and signs into candles and other objects. The effect is similar to that of the magic wand.

Ritual Dagger

The Tibetan ritual dagger (sketch at the right) is used for conducting energy and charging objects in the same way as the wooden knife. It consists of a brass-like link that makes it unsuitable as a defense against attackers from the world of spirits.

The dagger is charged with prana-energy (vital energy) or element powers (see Chapter "Magic Exercises"). With it, the shaman breathes cosmic energy into his body and then lets it flow through his fingers into the dagger. He repeats this procedure seven times in a row. The more often an object is charged, the stronger is its magical power.

The dagger shown carries the images of some gods. This links it to their power. It also means that the shaman is acting on behalf of these entities.

Athame

The classical Athame (picture on the right) is a tool from the European witch tradition. Many skilled sorcerers and witches prefer to craft it themselves. The handle is preferably black; the blade is of steel or iron and can be magnetized. If the knife is purchased commercially, it must first be thoroughly cleansed from foreign energies with water and incense.

According to Wicca tradition, the athame is charged as follows: The witch holds the knife with the blade pointing away from her. Then, she draws a magnet toward her alongside the blade. She repeats this charging at every new moon.

The charging can also be carried out in a completely individual manner—by charging the athame with prana-energy, for example, as described with the ritual dagger. And since the knife as a symbol is associated with the element of air, a charging with the fire-element is also recommended. The element of fire is breathed in from the cosmos and conducted with the hands into the athame. It is important for the witch to imagine the flame vividly and feel its energy. Here, too, several repetitions are in order.

As with all charged objects, the ritual knife should be wrapped in silk and stored carefully. An athame with a steel or iron blade can be utilized for many magic acts. Beyond the possibilities described for the wooden knife and ritual dagger, the athame also functions for defense and force. Appropriately charged, it can injure or even destroy spirit entities, and it can also force a spirit or demon to carry out an order.

The Sword

The sword is an important instrument for the calling of spirit entities, and indispensable for working with demons. An attacking demon can be hacked to pieces with its blade. Just the fact that a magician possesses such a sword elicits respect from many (mostly lower) entities. Often it is used to exact services from spirit entities, but this is a misuse of power, for most entities can be persuaded to perform services by offering a trade, an appropriate equivalent, or a sacrificial gift. They are then much easier to control. Exerting force on spirits always leaves you open to an unexpected attack.

As with the knives, the sword is most effective if the magician himself crafts it. The sword should have a length of 28 to 40 inches (70 cm to 1m). Ideally, the hilt should be made from highly conductive copper. Most important, however, is a blade of good steel into which the magician can engrave power symbols, runes, vévés, and the names of certain entities. The charging is done, as described for ritual knives, with prana- and/or fire energy. When charging, the magician uses his concentrated will to transfer all the desired attributes to the sword that is to embody strength, power, and victory.

A sword is splendidly appropriate for freeing oneself from the influences of foreign energies. To achieve this, the magician makes powerful strokes with the sword in the air around his head, while before his inner eye he cuts the threads that are connecting him to the undesirable energies.

The Trident

In significance and function, the trident corresponds to the sword, but its symbolic meaning is wider. Its three prongs signify the magician's ability to function equally well in all three areas—the spiritual, the energetic and the material. The trident is used primarily in contact with lower spirit entities and demons. Many fire spirits carry it as a symbol of the omnipotence of their element. Demons, too, often appear with a trident. It means that the entity has influence on all three levels.

To craft a trident, you need a wooden stick of the desired size to which you fasten a metal fork with three prongs of equal lengths. You can engrave the names of gods on all of them.

The charging is done in the same way as for ritual knives and swords. Like the sword, the trident is a weapon with which you can defend yourself or exert force.

The Wand

The wand is one of the most important symbols of the magic will. Its shape, the material used, and the accessories depend on the magician's special desires. The true power of the wand depends on its charge and equipment.

Shamans often work with unusually-formed wands in connection with crystals or animal attributes—these can be parts of animals, or the shape of the wand itself may correspond to an animal. The sketch to the left pictures such a wand, which carries a stronger natural energy because of its striking deformity. Shamans engage the special help of animal spirits when they use parts of the particular species for the crafting of magical implements.

European witches, on the other hand, use traditional, rather simple, plain wands made from certain woods. The sketch on the right shows such a wand. Made of a precious wood, it is in addition charged with energy through metal rings. The following woods are especially suited for wooden wands: oak, willow, hazel, elder, acacia, ash, and black thorn.

The sketch on page 165 shows a spiral-like winding rod in whose tip a crystal was inserted to bundle the energy. The natural form is reminiscent of a snake and embodies its energy. Such winding rods are used primarily for healing

purposes. They are a form of the staff of Ascle-
pius (the Caduceus—symbol of the personal
welfare professions, such as pharmacists and
physicians). Old vines and turned willow branches
are good for this purpose, especially the wood of
the willow, which is especially conductive. Hazel and
black thorn are also favored in the witch tradition. A
rod made from the wood of the elder bush is strongly
connected with saturnine energies (ruled by the planet
Saturn, which stands for seriousness and proximity to
nature) and is fashioned primarily for contact with
elementary entities and demons. A limb of the ash is used
in the healing of illnesses. The Druids (Celtic priests and
clairvoyants) thought that the oak was the tree with the
greatest power; equating its energy to the attributes of
Mars (among them, courage, achievement, capability).
It is desirable for strengthening the magician's will.

The length of the magic wand is the distance
between the elbow and the tip of the middle finger of
the magician. For healing, shorter rods from magnetized
metal or with a crystal tip are sometimes used. For
larger rituals, wooden or metal rods are used that may
be over 40 inches (1m) long. The radius should be at
least half an inch to 3/4 of an inch (1 to 2cm), and for
longer rods correspondingly more.

The Charging of Magic Wands

This practice is especially designed for magic wands, but
it can also be used in a modified form for charging other magical
objects.

Take the wand and concentrate on it. Imagine that you yourself are becoming the wand. Then, transfer your concentrated will into the wand and figure out how long you want the charge to last. You may decide that you want the energy to renew itself continuously and that the rod should recharge daily by itself. The wand can also be charged with other attributes. Your will, through concentration, may transfer such capabilities as the power of healing, clairvoyance, or power over animals. The procedure should take at least ten minutes.

The more often you repeat the charging, the more strength is gathered into the wand, which embodies your power. At first, with its help, you can influence the spiritual level, and later the energetic, and finally the material one. This effect will set in after the 462nd repetition of the magical charging, at the latest (462 is a numeral from the Kabbalah, a systematized secret magical system from the 12th century). Oriental magicians often perform a ritual 462 times in order to get it to manifest on the material level.

Magic rods can be charged with many different energies— which one depends on the personality of the magician and the purpose for which the rod is used. A rod can be charged with prana-energy (vital energy), as described on page 160 and in the chapter "Magic Exercises." If you want to work primarily with the powers of the elements (earth, fire, water, air), you can charge the wand with a single element or even with akasha, the fifth element, the ether. To do this, you must in each case imagine a universe that consists entirely of the chosen element. From that universe, you then draw the substance directly into the wand, without letting it flow through your own body, as is customary in other cases.

Unlike the other elements, the ether cannot be bound in a rod, but through frequent repetitions of the charging process, it may set causes in the primeval ground that can have results later. Rods that have been charged with akasha are especially powerful and command respect from many entities. Magicians, especially those who work with demons, usually prefer that kind of rod.

A thoroughly charged rod is also valuable if the magician will not be able to fully concentrate at the time of its use. The rod can also be taken along on trips to spiritual and energetic levels.

The charged wand is always carefully stored and usually wrapped in silk, so that its charge is protected and other people cannot come in contact with it.

The Witches' Wand

The wood is cut at the time of the full moon. The phase of the moon is significant, because it influences osmosis and thereby the energetic charging of the plants. Payment for the wand is made with a drop of your own blood.

Drill a hole into one end of the wand, put a drop of your blood on a small piece of cotton, and slip it into the hole in the wand. Then, seal the opening with candle wax. Next, with a knife, etch your sorceress name, preferably in runes, into the wax and draw a pentagram in front and behind it. At the new moon that follows the full moon, consecrate the wand with water, wine, and fire to the goddess Diana. Smudge (smoke) the wand with incense and then oil it, preferably with rose oil that is consecrated to Diana. The charging can be carried out as described earlier or according to your personal preferences.

Wooden Wand

Cut the wand from one of the woods named before. It's a good idea to consider the phases of the moon and astrology in order to determine the most favorable time, but not absolutely necessary, if you carefully charge the wand later. Removes the bark with a knife that is used exclusively for rituals. Then the names of gods or the gods' vévés can be etched into the wand.

The Metal Wand

Procure two different rods. One is for the emission of energy through electrical powers, the other for attracting the desired powers, thus receiving a magnetic charge. Such rods are very effective in practical work and must be charged in a special way.

A copper pipe with a radius of half to 3/4 of an inch (1 to 2cm) is needed for an electrical wand. Fill it with pulverized amber, an excellent conductor, and solder the ends closed. To charge the rod, take it into your right hand and imagine that you are in a universe of white-hot light. Allow yourself to feel the heat intensely, and the expanding power of this energy. Breathe it into your body through your lungs and pores, beginning with seven breaths. Then, while exhaling seven times, transfer the energy through your fingers into the rod. If necessary, the charging can be repeated. After the process is over, pay attention to your body to see that it has returned to normal. If it hasn't, just breathe until you feel normal again.

The magnetic wand is a steel rod with a length of 12 to 20 inches (30 to 50cm). Fill it with pulverized mountain crystals and then solder both ends. Take the rod into your left hand and imagine that you are in a universe consisting entirely of water. Concentrate on feeling the wetness and coolness on your skin and experience yourself as a dry sponge that is soaking up the water through your lungs and pores. By the power of your will, press the entire soaked-up energy through your fingers into the rod. It is sufficient to repeat the exercise seven times.

The charged wands are wrapped in silk for storage. For magic work, always hold the electric wand in your right hand, the magnetic one in your left.

The Pointer Wand

The magic pointer wand is the Haitian equivalent of the magic wand. With its help, energies are transferred from one place to another. It is also possible to catch spirits with the use of a pointer wand. You can buy these wands commercially. They are made of bamboo rods with a length of 16 to 20 inches (40 to 50cm). Before they can be used, they must be buried in the ground for one day and one night to receive the blessing of the earth spirits.

On one end of the rod, the foot of a black chicken is set in (see sketch) that has been ritually butchered with the Loa's permission. (The Loa gives permission if the chicken accepts the offered feed.) The food and some feathers are attached to the wand and wrapped with leather bands. Feathers are also attached in two or three more places. Tree sap serves as glue, since only natural materials may be used in the manufacture of the wand. A red silken band is tied around the wand close to its handle. Some wands are also equipped with the bones or skulls of other animals. The wand can be decorated with the vèvès of the Loa, as well as with the most important symbol of power, the Voodoo pentacle (see the chapter "Magic Symbols").

The Curse Wand

A curse wand is used for sending curses and for self-defense. The magician needs a strong rod at least 24 inches (60cm) long. After the loose bark is removed from the rod, he attaches the head of a horse made from wood or he carves into it the image of his enemy, showing him in an obscene posture. Then he carves the curse into the wand. It might read like this:

These three curses I am throwing at you and ▶▶▶ *threefold ice* |||.
May the 49 wild spirits plague you with sorrow and pain.
Hell is seizing your despicable soul and pulling you down!

He sticks the rod into the ground within sight of his enemy's house and directs it toward him. The deadly subterranean radiations of the goddess Hel are attracted through the rod, and they are directed onto the enemy through the head of the horse. The rod is placed around midnight on a waning moon.

The Chalice

The chalice is assigned to the element of water and may be used in all magic acts that are connected with water. It is, for example, indispensable in calling water spirits indoors (see the chapter "Demons, Elemental Spirits, Sphere Creatures"). In the Orient, it was used to influence weather and seafaring, and it is a symbol of wealth and abundance in the Western witchcraft tradition.

You can choose its form to suit your requirements. A simple wineglass or bowl is all you really need to represent the water element, but whatever the object is, it should be used only for purposes of magic. The more a magician occupies himself with magic, the more elaborate the chalice or the bowl that he works with, since they are objects whose workmanship also appeals to him. In rituals, the chalice or bowl is filled with fresh well or rainwater.

Clairvoyance

A glass chalice or bowl is used for purposes of clairvoyance. Fill it three quarters of the way with water and add purified crystals to increase its concentration. Keep a notebook and pen beside you.

Then sit in front of the bowl and breathe in and out deeply a few times, while your fingertips are touching the glass. Each time you exhale, hold your palms over the surface of the water and let your energy flow into the water through the tips of your fingers. Then place a candle next to the bowl and light it. Sit so that you can look through the glass at the surface of the water, while you continue to breathe calmly. Accept the images that rise out of the water without evaluating or organizing them, and if appropriate, take notes. The length of the ritual depends on you—quit when you get tired. The images are often continued in dreams later on. If the images were unpleasant, pour the water outside of your house or into the toilet. If they were pleasant, you can add it to a bath.

The Kettle

The sorcerer's kettle figures mainly in the female sorcerer tradition. It is generally made of copper or iron, and has a handle that is used to hang it over the fire. It is suitable for the preparation of magic beverages, witches' salves, and herbal brews, and may also be a receptacle for the burning of herbs.

The Lantern

The classic *laterna magica* has exchangeable panes through which light can be projected onto the wall. If you cannot find one, you can substitute a brightly colored glass behind which you place a candle.

In invocations, it is important to create a light that complements the vibration of the entity you are calling and thus facilitates the magic work. Red light can attract fire entities, whereas mermaids need green light (see the chapter "Demons, Elemental Spirits, Sphere Creatures"). Violet light is best for general magic work since its color vibration is neutral. This was already known to the Druids who preferred using it. Violet light also serves to prepare the consciousness for extrasensory perception. Entities of all kinds are comfortable in its vibration. There are just a few light-entities who prefer white light exclusively for their manifestations.

Incense Burning

Burning appropriate substances plays a great part in magic. It produces the vibrations needed in order to contact spirit entities. But these vibrations also stimulate the unconscious, helping you to develop special abilities. They can also bring about mind-altering conditions.

Burning Vessels

The choice of the receptacle used for burning is left up to you. It must, however, be always heatproof and insulated so that you can touch it and carry it. Its form must allow sufficient air to reach the burning substance. Natural receptacles are especially valuable. You can carry a sea sconce, for example, quite comfortably during the process without burning your fingers.

Use a feather to distribute the smoke. Birds are considered messengers from the world of spirits. With the help of their feathers, wishes and orders can therefore be directed to the appropriate entities. Feathers are especially well suited for freeing rooms of disturbing energies and unwanted entities. The trade in eagle feathers is forbidden, since these birds are protected, so feathers of the hawk or the buzzard are often used.

You can buy special charcoal on which to place incense. The burning material consists of those herbs and materials that are appropriate for the spirit entity that you are calling. If the spirit is to appear on the material level, smoke is an indispensable aid. With it, you can create the atmosphere that the spirit requires for its manifestation.

Smudging (Smoking) Materials

It is often wise to burn only one or two materials at the same time.
Mixtures can result in undesirable chemical reactions and cause
coughing or allergies.

Purpose	*Smudging Materials*
For improving the medium's abilities	Vermouth, celery seeds, cinnamon
To clearly receive dreams and visions	Mixture of red resin and aloe
To maximize money magic	Myrrh, saffron, labdanum or nutmeg, bay leaf, cedar
To increase a healing treatment's benefits	Rosemary, immortelle blossoms, eucalyptus, sandalwood
Protection against all kind of attacks	Mistletoe, mandrake, red sap, bay leaf, deadly nightshade
Cleansing from bad vibrations	Sage, sweet grass, blossoms and leaves of deadly nightshade eucalyptus, snakeskin
To increase your concentration	Labdanum, cinnamon, lavender
To increase your store of ideas	Bay leaf, cinnamon, myrrh, ginseng
To arouse love	Rose, jasmine, patchouli, musk
To further justice	Mixture of equal parts: labdanum and (in connection with a ritual) myrrh, frankincense, cedar, scotch pine

Magic Aids

To ban evil beings or harmful magic	St. John's wart (for invincibility), scotch pine, garlic, red resin, snakeskin
To facilitate astral travel	Lavender, sandalwood, mistletoe, violet roots, rose oil, patchouli
For better communication with other levels	Verbena, lotus, peppermint
For spiritual clarity	Mixture of equal parts of myrrh, hyssop, and lily

The Rattle

Rattles in various forms are usually used by shamans for calling spirits and eliminating illnesses. Here, too, the kind of rattle the shaman selects depends on how he intends to use it. He often prefers to make it himself from natural materials, or from items that have been in his family for a long time and are charged with the that energy. Such items also automatically establish a connection to the spirits of the ancestors. After the rattle is completed, it is magically charged by means of the imagination or by a traditional ritual. Depending on its proposed use, the rattle is then dedicated to a special spirit or god by a ritual or by attaching magic symbols.

In Africa, receptacles made of calabash, a melon plant, are very popular. Hollowed out, they make excellent rattles. As shown in the sketch above, a net was stretched over it, with kernels of seeds woven into it. These rattles serve many purposes such as the calling of spirits or the altering of your state of mind.

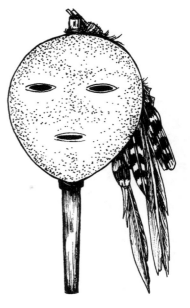

In South America, the use of melon plants is customary, as is illustrated in the sketch of the rattle (on the right), created by a shaman of the Caraja-Indians from Brazil. This one was filled with bean-like seeds. The attached feathers are meant to relay messages to the realm of the spirits. Therefore, these feathers come from birds that can be taught to speak or are known for their singing—parakeets, for instance, and canaries. Such a rattle is used primarily for calling spirits to a ritual.

Modern witches prefer using rattles like the antler-rattle shown below. Here, little bells and several feathers of a condor have been attached to the prongs of deer antlers, as in the rattles created by Native Americans. Such a rattle is called a "singing rod" and is used in healing rituals for chasing away illnesses.

The Flute

The shamans of many cultures use flutes to call the spirits. Depending on the materials used, the sound creates vibrations that can be perceived on the level of the spirit entities. In choosing an instrument, therefore, give special attention to the tone frequency and material. They should correspond to the elements or planets that belong to the entities you want to attract. Copper is suitable for Venus-beings, silver for the moon, wood for the air, and clay for the earth. Forest spirits are called with a Pan-type of flute, the spirits of the dead with a flute made from bone, and so forth. One-tone flutes are generally best for ritual invocations. Instruments made from bones or parts of animals have a strong connection to their spirits and powers. Most shamans take advantage of those energies that are already present. Like all other magic objects, the flute is charged according to the magician's needs before it is used. It is also consecrated, carefully stored, and used only for the purposes of magic.

Nigerian shamans use bone-flutes (sketch on the left) for healing. The flute shown here has in addition a carved wooden attachment in the form of a human head and is decorated with red seeds. The carved head lends fetish-character to the flute; most likely a spirit has been bound to it. The big hole in

the middle part serves for speaking invocation formulas into it, which are supposed to reach the spirits directly by changing the tone frequencies.

The flute made from a human thigh bone (shown on the left), was made by a Maschona medicine man from Zimbabwe. It is a ghost flute that is used to invoke spirits of the ancestors. Such flutes are also known in other parts of the world—in Tibet and Siberia, for instance—and they are also used for the ritual calling of the spirits of the dead.

Little flutes, similar to ocarinas, can be found in the South Pacific. The one shown here (see the sketch below) is made from a coconut and decorated with magic symbols that correspond to tattoos, typical for the area. The Maprik tribes use it for initiation rituals and fertility celebrations.

The Mirror

The magic mirror is a very practical help. With it, you can observe events in the far distance, and gain knowledge about past and future happenings. The mirror can be charged according to your needs and create visible and audible access to all levels, as well as make direct communication possible. Moreover, it can be used to charge a room with a distinct energy or to radiate yourself with it. Two magicians can also use it like a telephone.

As with most magical objects, a mirror should be made personally, if possible. A simple way to do it: Take sturdy cardboard and cut out the desired form (circle, square). Now cut the same form out of thick tissue paper. Spread a magic condenser (see page 184) on it several times. If you have decided on a solid condenser (pulverized metal), first apply a clear lacquer to the paper and then sprinkle the condenser on top. When the paper has dried well, glue it to the sturdy cardboard shape. You can also, of course, apply liquid and solid condenser to the mirror; this increases its effectiveness. Then cover it with black lacquer. It will be ready to use as soon as it has dried.

Another kind of mirror is the concave mirror, a rounded piece of glass that you can buy in a glass shop. Paint the side that is rounded on the outside with black paint (car paint, for instance). You may want to add a frame to the mirror to facilitate its use. If you want to add a condenser, cover the inner, rounded side of the glass with a clear paint and sprinkle some of the powder over it.

At this point you can prepare the mirror for the job at hand, or make several additional mirrors to use for different tasks. As with all magic objects, the mirror should be wrapped in a silk cloth, and stored safely when it is not needed.

Preparation of the Mirror

Sit down in front of the mirror and imagine on its surface a simple object, and also a form. Then, gradually proceed to more and more multi-layered forms. Make sure that you really see the object and push aside all unwanted pictures that might appear. In this way, you get your eyes adjusted to working with the mirror.

One-Time Mirror

Take a mirror with a slightly raised edge and pour some water on it. Add a few drops of the magic condenser (see page 184). Then, place the mirror on the ground in front of you. Place a candle or a magic lantern (see page 172) beside it. Now charge the surface as desired, or look into the mirror without any special goal, trying to remain free of thoughts about the evolving images.

Establishing Contact

If you want to establish contact with a person who is far away, charge the mirror with the fifth element, the ether. Do the basic inhaling (See the chapter "Magic Exercises") inside your body and conduct the energy into the mirror with your hands or the sun spectrum (solar plexus, lower end of chest bone). Just imagine that there is nothing but ether between you and the person you want to contact. Then the connection is established. In the same way, you can make contact with dead people or spirit entities of other levels.

Don't be discouraged by failures at the beginning. Continual practice will lead to success.

Seeing Pictures

If you want a picture to appear that is visible to the eyes of your material body, charge the mirror with the element earth (see the chapter "Magic Exercises"). In this case, let it flow directly from the cosmos into the mirror. Then fill your body and the room with the element of ether. After that, you can begin with the invocation of the spirit that you want to see. Address the mirror and mentally send into it the entity's vèvè and its qualities. In this manner, you establish contact. You can, in the same way, also establish a reference to past and future events and use the mirror as a kind of television screen for observing them.

If you are going to have the mirror aid in the invocation of the spirit entity, place it above the tip of a magic triangle (see the chapter "Magic Symbols").

Expansion

If you want to expand certain characteristics or abilities you already possess, charge the mirror with light. Sit in a relaxed position in front of the mirror and imagine the cosmic ocean of light. Scoop out the light from that ocean and let it flow into your mirror. At the same time, with high concentration, place into the mirror the wish that it expand the characteristic or ability in question. Then determine the span of time during which the expansion should take place. End the process when you see the power of light emanating from the mirror—or feel it in your body.

Then place the charged, open mirror down in your place of ritual or on your altar, or in your bedroom, where you will be radiated by the energies in your sleep. Usually, you cover a working mirror, but in this case, the mirror can be used open.

Travels

Sit in a relaxed position, fill yourself with the element of ether (see the chapter "Demons, Elemental Spirits, Sphere Creatures"), and conduct it with your fingers into the mirror. Repeat this procedure several times until you experience a feeling of being outside of space and time. Divert your attention from your body and totally concentrate on your spirit. Then, in your imagination, shrink yourself in so that you can move through the mirror to the energy level. At first everything may appear dark to you, but soon you will begin to perceive your environment and other beings. If you wish, you can also fetch certain entities by mentally calling their names into the ether.

When you are ready to end the process, leave the mirror in the same way you entered it and make sure that a good feeling returns to your body. If you do not feel good, get in touch with Mother Earth—by breathing deeply, by eating something earthbound (like potatoes), and by reestablishing inner and outer contact with your surrounding world.

In this way, you can visit all levels. Take care that when you are working in elementary levels (see the chapter "Demons, Elemental Spirits, Sphere Creatures") or spheres of the planets that the mirror is not charged with the element of ether, but with the element that corresponds with each realm—with the power of light that belongs to the planet. If, for example, you want to enter the realm of the water nymphs, charge the mirror with the water element. Then induce in yourself the feeling of *being* a water nymph, while you are entering that realm. It is then easy to get into contact with the water entities.

Magic Condensers

Condensers are used to energetically increase the power of magic charges of all kinds. There are two kinds—solid (pulverized) and liquid. They are used universally, and can be employed to increase the charge of various magic implements. In earlier times, they were kept strictly secret.

Solid (Pulverized) Condensers

The solid (pulverized) condenser, the electromagicum that was used by ancient alchemists, consists of a melted mixture of 30g silver, 30g gold, 15g copper, 15g quicksilver, 6g tin, 5g lead, and 3g iron. You can reduce this formula proportionately, if necessary. Magic bells or mirrors can be cast from this mixture.

Electromagicum can also be mixed in dry form from the powders of the metals described above in the appropriate proportions. If the metals are not available in powder form, you can scrape them off a piece of the metal with a file. Quicksilver, which is liquid by nature, is bound to an amalgam by the heating process.

Liquid Condenser

The simplest liquid condenser can be made from a brew of certain plants. Especially suitable are white lilies (blossoms, roots and leaves), mandrake roots, arnica blossoms, and genuine chamomile. In addition, a gold tincture is needed, which you can obtain in a pharmacy. Preparations from gold are used in homeopathy; for the preparation of condensers, a potency of D1-D3 is recommended. If only a higher potency is available, you would need to increase the other ingredients proportionately.

Put a handful of the selected plants in a pot and cover them with water. Cover the pot and boil for 20 minutes. Then let the brew cool and filter it through a fine strainer or filter paper. Heat the liquid once more until it has been reduced to approximately 100ml. When is has cooled, add 20 drops of the gold tincture. If you are just going to use the condenser for your own purposes, add some drops of your own blood. Pour the liquid into a darkly colored bottle and add the same quantity of a high-content alcohol. Shake the bottle well. The condenser will keep and be effective for many years due to the alcohol content. Store it in a dark and not too warm place.

The Bell

Some sorcerers, especially in the Orient, use the rhythmic chiming of a magic bell to get the attention of the spirits in a certain sphere of planets. The number of chimes is coordinated with the corresponding number of the sphere. The bell is manufactured of electromagicum, the solid condenser that contains all the metals of the various planets.

Voodoo Rituals

Amulets

T hrough amulets you can establish contact with the energies and powers of particular entities. Some examples of amulets and talismans that have proven successful are described here. Preferably, they are to be homemade. If you buy an amulet, regardless of whether it is a stone or a piece of metal, you must purify it of foreign energies before using it. The best way to do this is to put the object in a glass of cold, clean water for three days. Objects that do not tolerate water can be placed between mountain crystals, or hematite drum stones, in order to purify them. The amulet is then effective under its own power, or you can charge it with a desired goal in mind.

Charging an Amulet

It is easiest to charge the amulet or talisman by repeated invocations depending on its intended purpose. Clearly state the order, and repeat it continuously in the same words.

If the amulet works through the powers of the elements, the elements must be accumulated (see the chapter "Magic Exercises"). You can also charge the talisman by means of the power of light or prana. To do this, proceed in the same way that you would when charging other magic objects. Inhale white light from the cosmos with total concentration, and while exhaling, transmit the desired qualities (protection, wealth, health, spiritual abilities, etc.) in the stream of light through your fingers into the amulet. Each repetition of the procedure increases the charge. You can also adjust the object so that its power increases daily through ever-present vital powers. If you want to prepare a talisman for another person, don't let the energy flow through your own body, but take it directly out of the cosmic ocean of light.

186

A talisman can be nothing more complicated than a piece of paper to which the entity's vèvè is attached, but it can be more complex (see the examples that follow). Whatever form you choose, attach the vèvè to the talisman in some way—by carving, painting, etc. You can then charge it in the appropriate ritual. To do this, draw the vèvè of the entity on the ground, place the talisman on it, and surround the vèvè with symbols and sacrificial objects. Then draw a circle around it, put candles around it in suitable colors, and light them (see the chapter "Working Magic"). You might also burn incense (see pages 174–175 to choose the right type).

Then point to the talisman with the magic wand and ask the entity to charge it with its power. Leave the talisman in the circle for a few days. Then thank the entity and let it go. Remove the circle, the vèvè, and the sacrificial offerings from the ritual place.

Carry the talisman with you in a pocket on the left side of your body. It is not advisable to connect yourself with an entity in this way for a long period of time; it can lead to a strong dependency.

Examples of Some Effective Amulets and Talismans

Amulet for Success

The bindrune (rune combination) pictured here signifies success and goal-oriented action on all levels. Engrave it into clay or wood and paint it with a red color or blood. If you use animal blood for the coloring, it will change the energy of the amulet, which could result in advantages or disadvantages.

Talisman for the Fulfillment of Wishes

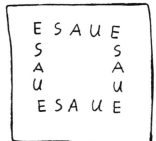

```
E  S  A  U  E
S           S
A           A
U           U
E  S A  U  E
```

Write on a piece of paper with blood from your left hand the magic square, ESAUE, as shown at the right. While writing, with your imagination, place your most longed-for wish in the middle of the square. Carry the piece of paper in a small pouch on your body, perhaps on a chain around your neck until the wish is fulfilled. This is a very powerful talisman.

Good Luck Charm

This talisman is similar to a medicine pouch. Its contents depend on its intended purpose, but it should contain a plant, a mineral, and an item of animal origin. They should be appropriate to the task: If the talisman, for example, is to attract love, fill it with rosebuds, rose quartz (or perhaps a ruby), and the feather of a turtle dove. In addition, it is useful to add some food for the spirit entities, such as maize kernels or Tonka beans.

You might want to try the following combination for a lucky charm:

A piece of gold (a coin, for example), a white feather, a piece of coal and a mountain crystal, dust from an altar, and a pheasant eye from a taxidermist. Put all the ingredients into a white small bag made from a natural material and carry it with you.

Talisman for Swiftness

The flying bird connects the wearer with the qualities of the element air. It lends speed and lightness. If possible, it should be made of silver or light enamel. It is an effective charm if things have to be carried out quickly.

Lucky Charm for Strengthening a Love Relationship

You need three satin ribbons in rose, white, and lilac, each 15 inches (38cm) long. Tie the ribbons together in a knot and braid them, while asking Aphrodite (Venus) for support. Tie the ends into a knot also. Then, wind the braid around a vanilla-bean pod and fasten it well. Keep the talisman under the bed or under your pillow. It serves to make love last. Put together the lucky charm on Valentine's Day or on a Friday during the waxing moon.

Stone Amulets

Stones and crystals are superbly suited as amulets. It's especially important to clean them regularly in a water bath, since minerals strongly absorb disturbing energies. Choose a stone that is suited for the task:

- Turquoise protects against spiritual attacks and negative spirit entities.
- Labradorite prevents spiritual as well as physical attacks.
- Mountain crystal provides clarity and harmony.
- Rose quartz possesses rejuvenating and harmonizing qualities.
- Amber attracts happiness and wealth and lends lightness at work.
- Dumortierite gives richness of ideas.
- Magnetite cleanses body and spirit from foreign energies. (This mineral may not come into contact with water, but must be recharged between hematite drum stones.)
- Sugelite protects against serious illnesses such as cancer and AIDS.

The Divining Rod

The common divining rod consists of a forked branch of the hazel bush. Wood of the willow tree or a young oak shoot is also used at times. Before working with the rod, put it into water so it will retain its flexibility. In addition to the traditional search for water and for the detection of metals and mineral deposits, the divining rod is also used in magic work. You can locate fields of disturbance and suitable places for rituals with it. Particularly advantageous are places at which two powerful energies intersect. With the rod, it is easy to follow the course of these channels.

While divining with the rod, the two equally long ends (see the sketch below) are grasped from below or from above, so that the ends run between the ring and little fingers. This grasp prevents an involuntary twitching of the little finger, which could falsify the result. The ends of the rod bend apart with easy pressure. The rod is always held parallel to the ground while you're walking. If it is deflected, the tip of the rod can move upward as well as down.

The rod can be used in many ways. During a search, it is important to fully concentrate on the kind of energy that you want to find. By the way, almost all people possess sufficient sensitivity to employ a divining rod successfully.

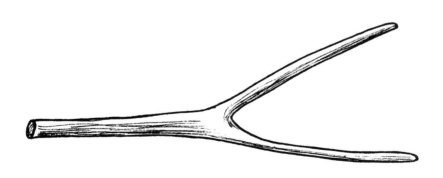

In addition to the forked divining rod, you might want to try a two-part metal rod. You can make it easily from two thin metal clothes hangers (see the sketch below). It is especially good for measuring the aura (the invisible energy field that surrounds living beings and objects), and detecting other energy fields. A metal rod has also the advantage of not becoming warped and not being subject to the energetic oscillations of a wooden rod.

To craft a metal rod, pinch open the top of a metal clothes hanger with a pair of pliers. You want to achieve an L-form. To do this, bend the hanger open and cut it to a length that is convenient to hold in your hand. Follow the same procedure with the second hanger. Then hold both wires parallel to each other. Your grasp must be loose enough that the rods can move freely. Energy fields will be indicated either by an intersecting or a bending outward of the tips of the wires. Try it out. Most people are able to use this kind of rod.

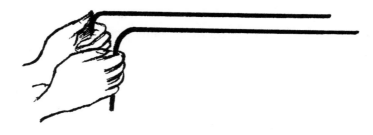

The Pendulum

The pendulum is also very useful in magic work. For one thing, you can use it to test the strength of energetic power fields and magic objects. You can also use it as an intermediary to establish contact with spirit entities. If you wish to test whether an object is suitable for a certain magic job, hold the pendulum in your right hand, between your open left palm and the object. If the direction of the movement is back and forth between your hand and the object, the object is suited to the task. If the movement, however, is lateral, it is not. Since at times the movements of the pendulum may differ from the general rule, it's essential to consult the pendulum as to what the movements mean before you start.

Connection to the Spirit Guardian

If you don't have a common form of pendulum (see the sketch on the following page), a wedding ring or even a nut to which a string is fastened, can serve in its place. Wind the string around your index finger so that the pendulum can hang down freely about 8 inches (20cm). Then comfortably support your right elbow on a table, and place your left hand on the tabletop. To start with, create a trance-like condition by breathing deeply into your stomach cavity and eliminating thought as best you can. Then, move the hand that is holding the pendulum so that it feels independent of your material body. The procedure is a little like taking off a piece of clothing. It is done by imagining the procedure with your concentrated will. The energetic hand is then willfully placed on the table. Now, the hand with the pendulum has been freed for immediate use by a spirit entity.

With this practice it is advisable to establish contact only with your own spirit guardian, since inexperienced people can easily become victims of an unwanted possession.

Ask your spirit guardian to communicate through the pendulum. Here, too, it's a good idea to ask first which movement will indicate a "Yes," and which one will mean a "No" or a "Perhaps." As an additional help, you could set up a sounding device that the pendulum can strike, with the number of strokes relating to the answer. Other possible aids are pendulum diagrams with letters, numbers and words.

Automatic writing or working with an ouija board functions in the same way. Since the possibility of an entity taking hold of your hand is unlikely, the danger of a possession is smaller than with an invocation. Yet, here too, caution is warranted.

Nails

In Africa, and also in other witchcraft circles, the use of iron nails has a long tradition. Since iron and steel can penetrate even spiritual energies, they are superbly suited to be effective on this level. Your success with them depends on your goal.

Before using it, charge the nail with the desired power. This takes place through concentration—addressing the nail and magnetizing it. The latter is carried out with the aid of a magnetic rod that you stroke over the nail in the direction of your body, until the nail is magnetized. Prepared like this and accompanied by magic formulas, the nail is slowly driven into the ground at a place of power at the appropriate time. Places of power are old cult areas such as stone circles, prehistoric graves, cemeteries, or the location of an old chapel. In nature, power places are springs; oak groves; witches' circles; where poisonous mushrooms grow in a circle; crossroads; and areas that are conspicuous by special ground and stone formations.

During the time of the Romans, witches used bronze nails that were sometimes decorated with magic signs and symbols. The one above shows a snake and various other signs.

Shamans work with nails for the purpose of healing. If the sick person is suffering from a head ailment, the shaman uses a pecan or a walnut (see the sketch below), whose kernels are reminiscent of a brain, which makes them suitable for this technique. First, the shaman establishes an energetic connection between the sick person and the nut. This can be accomplished by touch. Then the nail is pushed through the nut and the ailment driven out.

The nail fetish is known in central Africa where it plays a large role in healing and harmful magic. It is a figure that has a hollow space inside with a door in the back. This cavity serves either as a container for a spirit, or for herbs that are put inside to strengthen the sorcery. The nails are driven into the hollow figure, while the sorcerer speaks the invocation. Usually there is a mirror on the front side that can transfer the magic onto the person targeted.

The Voodoo Needle

This is a useful tool in doll magic (see page 85). The basis is a steel needle approximately 6 inches (15 cm) long, onto which a shorter piece of a thin bamboo rod is attached. A small wooden bead and some feathers are attached to the upper end of the bamboo rod. It is preferable to use feathers from a ritually killed chicken.

Common needles and nails (see page 195) can, of course, also be used for doll magic, but the Voodoo needle is easier to heat over the fire. Bokors, black magic practitioners who carry out harmful magic acts, use this procedure to cause greater sufferings to their victims.

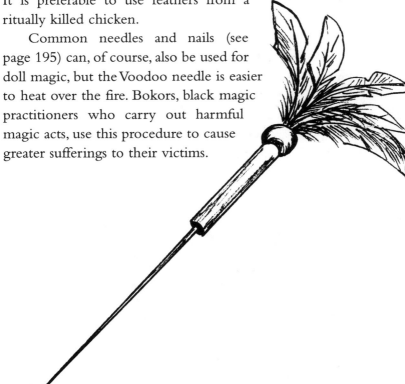

Masks

Masks are found all over the world in almost every culture. Originally, they had a ritual meaning. In most cases, they represent supernatural beings or spirits. A magician who works with masks first informs himself fully about the qualities of the entities that the mask embodies, for he will have to control these powers when he calls them.

Masks worn for ritual purposes go through a careful manufacturing process. Color and appearance must correspond to the spirit entity portrayed. There are often old models that must be followed exactly, even if only to avoid angering the spirit. In addition, the mask is adorned with accessories—parts of animals and plants that belong to the spirit's area of power. Typical headgear and symbols are also added. After its completion, the mask is consecrated to the spirit

entity or the god for whom it was created in a more or less elaborate ritual, through which it is connected to the spirit's energy.

In order to complete the appearance, the mask is usually worn with appropriate clothing. Once the wearer of the mask is in his costume, he abandons, so-to-speak, his own being. During the ceremony, he embodies only the godly entity and acts on its behalf. Actually, the bearer of the mask fuses with the spirit so strongly that he assumes its demeanor and even takes on supernatural powers that he does not possess in his daily life. He becomes the godly entity's surrogate. Such performances generally go on for a fairly limited time.

Besides the great face masks, there are smaller masks that are made for magic purposes. They, too, are connected with the entities whom they symbolize and embody their power in the material world. Amulets in the form of masks can be worn for protection on a chain around the neck.

The Tlingit Indians from the Northwest use masks for chasing away illnesses. The mask shown on page 198 carries with it the traits of an eagle. Its head ornament is made up of various white condor and magpie feathers.

The meaning of some masks is not known; even where the culture is still in existence. There are tribes that do not pass along this knowledge. The Malangan in the South Pacific use masks that resemble a boar's head (see the sketch on page 199). It is likely that such masks directly embody the spirit of the animal represented, or a spirit entity that has similar qualities and to whom the animal species is assigned. Hogs are of great ritual significance in the South Pacific; they are the embodiment of prosperity throughout the entire region.

7.
Magic Exercises

Relaxation

This exercise increases the flow of energy and brings about a better body consciousness. You can do it while sitting or reclining, but don't fall asleep.

First, the whole body is relaxed step-by-step, beginning at the feet. All the parts of the body become very heavy. When you arrive at the head, totally relax and loosen all your facial muscles. Your breathing should be long and deep.

To further deepen your relaxation at the end of the exercise, strongly tighten all your muscles, including the facial ones, and after a few seconds, relax them all at once. This is also an effective way to release muscle sprains.

Breathing

Deep breathing is a very important exercise. It connects us to life and to the energies that surround us. Vital energy is absorbed through the lungs, and poisonous substances expelled. Deep, quiet, even breathing is recommended to everyone. As will be discussed later in the section on Pranayama (page 204), astonishing results can be achieved simply through practicing one of these breathing techniques.

Deep Breathing

First push the air out of your lungs from below to above. Pull in your stomach muscles, then your chest muscles. When you inhale, first relax your stomach muscles again and then your chest muscles, so that your lungs fill with air from below to the top. Since the lungs are organs of negative pressure, only exhaling involves effort. The process of inhaling happens by itself. When you breathe deeply, your lungs completely fill with air down to the lowest tip, which guarantees the greatest possible supply of oxygen.

Alpha Breathing

The alpha state, a condition of a heightened and, at the same time, complete relaxation, can be achieved with alpha breathing. The feeling of lightness and perception is greatly increased. The phases during which the breath is held—or not allowed in—result in a disengagement from the material level, since no exchange of energy is taking place.

Begin with deep breathing (see above). After a few breaths, concentrate on your heartbeat, or feel your pulse. When you locate your pulse, inhale during the next four pulse beats—then hold your breath for two additional pulse beats. Exhale during the following four pulse beats—and remain for two beats without air. Limit this exercise to about ten minutes in the beginning. You can later extend it as desired.

If the rhythm of 4–2–4–2 feels uncomfortable, you can change it as you want. With 2–2–2–2 or 4–4–4–4, or 6–4–4–4, you can achieve the same effect. You can increase the breathing phases as you like, with the growing capacity of your lungs. Make sure that you are not overburdening your lungs. Your breath should flow calmly and deeply, without your face getting flushed or your muscles getting cramped.

Alpha breathing can be practiced very well by breathing in the rhythm of your steps while taking a leisurely walk. Here too, avoid overdoing it, which could lead to an unpleasant muscular stiffness.

Pranayama

Prana is Sanskrit and means life, the all-present, universal vital energy. All bodies on all levels are formed from this energy. Mastery and control of prana energy can therefore decisively influence body and soul. Pranayama means "the elongated breath," which will be self-explanatory as you read on.

The exercise consists of single steps that are built upon each other. Begin with Step 1 and gradually work your way up until you master the whole sequence. The inhaled prana has the form of a white, glowing gas that fills the whole cosmos.

Step 1: At the beginning, induce the alpha condition with a few breaths (page 203). Then, continue, but keep clearly in your concentrated imagination the idea that prana is flowing into your body—all the way into the tips of your fingers and into your toes. When you feel that energy, the goal of the exercise has been reached.

Step 2: With the aid of your will power, pull down the stream of prana along your spine while you inhale. Then when you hold your breath, let the energy run up and down your spine several times. Strongly tighten the sphincter, and push upward from the coccyx. To push it down, relax and tighten your neck muscles. Then, when you exhale, only air will be expelled; the prana will remain in your body. In the beginning, don't extend this exercise past seven breaths, since it results in a strong energetic charge to which your body must gradually become accustomed.

Step 3: You are now learning to control the prana stream, through which illnesses can be cured and spiritual powers developed. While you inhale, the energy is drawn into the "sun lattice" (the solar plexus, at the lower end of your chestbone), and is being formed into a shining ball. When you hold your breath, this ball is sent to a spot that needs strengthening. When you exhale, the ball of light is left there. Here, too, seven repetitions are sufficient.

For the purpose of self-healing, send the prana ball to the place of sickness and saturate it with imagined health and recovery. To obtain spiritual abilities, guide the prana ball from the sun lattice along the spine up to the basis of the skull. While you hold your breath, let this area be powerfully flooded and insert into it your desire—for clairvoyance, for example, keenness of hearing, and so on.

Step 4: In order to increase the effect, you can vary the breathing technique after some time: While inhaling, close the right nostril with your finger so that the prana and breath can enter only through your left nostril. After holding your breath, hold your left nostril closed with your finger and exhale through the right one. This practice promotes a strong increase in the flow of energy.

This form of breathing can also be used for the fulfillment of wishes. While the inhaling of prana takes place through your left nostril, formulate your desire in your mind in clear words. During the holding of the breath, send the prana ball from the sun lattice to the brain. At the same time, create a vivid picture of what it will be like when your wish has become a reality. Then, exhale through your right nostril, fully convinced that the wish has already been fulfilled. This exercise, too, is repeated seven times.

Follow the same procedure if you want to send the prana stream to charge a magic object. The difference is that you will be sending the collected energy out from your body through your hands or fingers while you exhale.

When you want to transfer the prana to others, don't let the energy run through your own body. Send the prana directly out of the cosmos into the other body by virtue of your will and imagination.

Pores or Skin Breathing

Pores or skin breathing results in a strong energetic charging of your whole body. It is best to lie on your back for this exercise. While you inhale, you not only pull the prana energy with full concentration through your lungs into your body, but also through your skin, through all the pores of your body. While you hold your breath, imagine that your whole body is completely filled with white light. Then exhale normally. Repeat this exercise seven times.

Trance

Trance can be achieved in different ways. Generally, a certain uniformity of sounds, movement, and thought is created that largely shuts off the intellect. Through entering inner peace, the consciousness moves into the threshold condition between waking and sleeping. In this state, people are especially receptive to perceptions from other levels, since changes take place in their own vibrations and sense of time.

In Haiti, trance is often created through certain drum rhythms. Damballah's snake dance, for example, may bring it about. In technologically advanced cultures opportunities for trance may not be widespread, but there still are many ways to induce it.

Timeless and Spaceless

Get into a comfortable position and begin inhaling, deeply and slowly, into your stomach cavity. Keep concentrating on your breathing. By that means alone, you will attain a trancelike condition. If thoughts arise, let them fall away and immediately redirect your attention to your breathing.

To help defer disturbing thoughts, you may want to choose a mantra. A "mantra" is a mystical word formula that facilitates meditation. The Buddhist mantra "Om" is recommended, and if you prefer, you can recite it in its full length version, "Aum mani padre hum," which means "Jewel in the Lotus Flower," representing the perfection of Buddha and his teachings. You can also reach a trancelike condition with the mantra "Shutati shumavi," since it has no meaning in any language. Repeat the mantra in your mind or speak it loudly until a complete void of thought has been achieved.

Instead of using a mantra, you can shut off your thoughts by continually staring at one point. This, in addition, is a good concentration exercise. The point should not be up so high that your eyes begin to tear.

Concentrate again on your breathing and aim to maintain a condition of complete relaxation. When you feel timeless and spaceless, the goal has been reached. You can increase the duration of the exercise from a few minutes to an hour.

Shamans of many cultures follow another procedure that is very effective. They attain a trance-like condition through making a steady movement back and forward, or a circling movement of the upper body, that eliminates the earth element.

Programming the Unconscious

Autosuggestion is a simple and effective technique for change. The human unconscious learns through repetition. In order to reach a goal, you repeat an idea to yourself over and over again until it is accepted as reality by the brain.

It is important to use short, comprehensible words in the present tense. If, for example, you want to develop the ability to consciously remember dreams, the affirmation could be: "After awakening, I remember all details of my dreams." The formula may not contain any negations or wish formulations, such as "I would like to/will/wish." If you want to get rid of something, the affirmation would describe what it will be like when you are free of it. So, instead of "I will not be fearful," you would say: "I am courageous." In order to successfully influence the unconscious, you need to formulate your desired state precisely, present it to yourself as an order, and then follow a rigorous program of repetition.

Once you have decided on an affirmation, repeat it 20 to 40 times before you fall asleep. The space between waking and sleeping is particularly good for a connection with the unconscious. Repeat the exercise immediately after waking up, and success will soon arrive.

The programming should always contain only one precise idea at a time and should be retained no longer than 60 days. After this time, the thought has certainly entered the unconscious. The actualization of the idea may become evident before the end of this time period, but it may also do it later, after the brain has established the necessary preconditions. All powers serving spiritual advancement can be developed in this manner.

Strengthening the Willpower

All exercises that help you master bodily functions and instincts strengthen the willpower. Various techniques can be used:

Fasting

It is not important to go without any food for days or weeks at a time. In the beginning, it is sufficient not to satisfy your emerging hunger immediately, but simply to prolong the time before you take in any food. The same applies to the desire for liquids. Addictions can also be controlled in this manner. After some practice, a few days of complete fasting can be achieved easily.

Abstention

Although it is desirable to control sexual urges, celibacy should not become a permanent condition. A more or less long period of sexual abstention is sufficient. The ultimate aim is to cease being a slave to your own cravings and to learn to willfully control and master your needs and feelings. In most cultures, the performance of a ritual is preceded by a preparation phase of fasting and abstention.

Holding Still

Another technique of developing the willpower is to remain in a certain posture over a period of time. This is done in some yoga exercises or in the Zazen exercise (sitting in the lotus position with legs crossed for several hours) in Zen Buddhism. Prolonged sitting in a meditative posture, with your legs crossed or on your heels, effects a strengthening of the willpower. When the position is beginning to get unpleasant, the idea is to prolong the duration of the exercise. Your body slowly will become accustomed to following the orders of the brain.

Visualization

One of the basic requirements for magic work is a well trained imagination—an ability to envision things in all their detail and to see them vividly with the inner eye. Here are some exercises that will help you to enhance this ability:

The Candle

Sit on the ground in a comfortable position and place a candle in front of you. Light the candle and look into the flame for a minute. Finally, close your eyes and cover them with both hands. Your goal is to continue seeing the flame before your closed eyes. If the picture drifts away, pull it back immediately. The exercise lasts for two minutes.

Forms

Begin by visualizing simple shapes—a red pyramid, for example, a yellow ball, or a white square. At the start, keep your eyes closed during the exercise. Later, project the images into the room with open eyes. Once you accomplish this, you can progress to more complicated forms and finally to living beings. The highest stage is the projection of a whole landscape before the spiritual eye.

The Knot

This third method is an excellent preparation for magic work: Sit down in the usual exercise position with eyes closed. Then, imagine two cords and tie them together in a knot. Choose a knot that you are skilled in using. If you're successful, repeat the exercise with your eyes closed.

In order to fine-tune your ability in visualization, try the next two exercises in which all senses are trained simultaneously.

Rocks

Envision yourself on a beach with a rocky coast. Lift one piece of rock, being distinctly aware of its weight. Now see yourself lift it over your head and throw it with full force far into the sea. Select a much heavier rock, inhale deeply, and lift it up. While exhaling, let this rock fly off with even greater ease. Continue this as long as you like. You have reached your goal when the vision feels as real as possible. In this way, you are preparing your spirit for the emission of magic energies.

Apple

For this second technique, envision an apple. Imagine taking it in your hand and looking at it from all sides, while distinctly noticing its scent. Then, take a hearty bite into it. The sound and the taste should be most distinct and prominent. Eat the whole apple, swallowing it a piece at a time, experiencing all the perceptions of the various senses. When only the core is left, the exercise is finished.

Mastering Thoughts

People of Western culture find it especially difficult to master the flood of thoughts that are always streaming in. But there are some exercises that can help you to accomplish this:

Breathing

The simplest exercise is to concentrate on the flow of your breath. Then, formulate and spiritually retain a particular thought, like a mantra (see page 207).

Do the exercise for five to ten minutes.

Void

In another technique, you create a complete void of thoughts. During this exercise, every thought that arises must be energetically rejected. If you succeed in maintaining this condition for ten minutes, you have reached the goal.

Attention

Steady observation of your thoughts is useful for an enlargement of your consciousness. Turn your attention to your own patterns of thought. If, for example, such formulas appear as "I am afraid" or "I can't do it," you need to change them immediately into their positive opposite, namely, "I am courageous," and "I can do it." You can use this exercise at any time. It sharpens your perceptions and strengthens your willpower.

Mind Reading

Reading the mind of others is an ability that is quite easy to attain. A prerequisite, though, is the ability to master your own thoughts. To receive the thoughts of another person, you must first erase every thought of your own. Then, you can direct your attention to the other person, open your spirit, and wait. The thoughts that impose themselves from outside, will, with some certainty, be coming from the target person. Distance does not matter in this case.

It is very important to learn to distinguish between your own thoughts and the thoughts of others. This is an essential requirement if you want to establish a connection with spirit entities, since communication with them, especially at the beginning, often takes place as telepathic perceptions.

Telepathy

Ask a friend for help with this exercise. First, select a picture or a thought that you want to communicate. Then, imagine the back of the target person's head (distance plays no role here) and, with full concentration, send the picture/thought into his brain. Now, you can find out whether the telepathy has been successful. Don't let failures at the beginning discourage you.

A different type of telepathic communication is carried out in the following manner: Sit on a chair and picture the person with whom you want to communicate sitting opposite you, as exactly and lively as possible. When you have the feeling of being connected with the person, you can talk to him or her and convey the information you choose.

Telepathy can also be used very successfully in healing treatments. Pictures that induce healing can be directly transferred into the unconscious of the sick person.

It is self-evident that telepathy must be used very carefully. A misuse of this power will always revert to the sender and impede his own development.

Clairvoyance

The development of clairvoyance generally takes place in two stages. The ability to foresee is mostly acquired with the inner eye, before you experience such perceptions with the material eye.

Average people possess only a limited range of vision that lies in the area between infrared and ultraviolet. Other vibrational areas are hidden from them, but animals have the ability to perceive them. This ability can be relearned and is supported by the following exercise:

Mirror

All objects with a shining surface, such as crystals, mirrors, and objects made of metal are suitable for the training of clairvoyant abilities. Do this exercise in the evening or in a darkened room.

A source of light, like a candle or a low lamp, is placed behind the back of your friend. Then, put a shining object on a black piece of cloth at eye level in front of yourself. Hold the object firmly in view, so the condition of a "void of thought" is created (see the corresponding exercise on page 213). With persistent practice, pictures of other places and people will appear after some time.

Another method is looking into a mirror and viewing water, as described in the chapter "Magic Aids." Work with the magic mirror also supports the development of this ability.

In order to achieve success quickly with these exercises, you can also employ the technique of pranayama, which was described before. Here, the inhaled prana is conducted into the eyes and accumulated there.

Inner Hearing

Inner hearing functions in much the same way as clairvoyance. At first, the ability of inner hearing is aroused, which later turns into hearing with the material ear. This sense is often quite well developed in primitive peoples.

Cosmic Murmur

Quiet and solitude are requirements for using the following technique. The night hours are best suited for it. Before beginning, stuff some cotton or a small piece of wax into your ears. Then, inhale prana energy a few times (see "Pranayama" exercise) into the area of your head. Now, calm your thoughts and listen attentively to the stillness. At first, a stronger rustling will become noticeable, out of which eventually voices and words can be heard. The perception at first is similar to a kind of loud thinking. With regular exercise, the ability will finally transfer to the material ear. Then, complete stillness will no longer be required in order to perceive tonal occurrences on the energetic level.

To achieve quick success, use a seashell. This is an exercise often practiced by the Tibetan monks. Hold the shell to one ear, while the other ear is closed with a wad of cotton or piece of wax. Your concentration will be focused on the murmuring of the shell, which will increase the sound of the ether.

A warning:
Friendly beings are not the only ones who dwell in other worlds. Until you have enough experience to distinguish between the various entities, look very critically at the messages you receive.

Spiritual Perception

This ability is used to perceive energetic vibrations and the presence of spirit entities. Psychometry also belongs to this area. It is possible to touch an object and have all connections to the object become evident.

Lie down on your back and consciously follow the flow of your breath. Then, with a strong determination to obtain clear perception, pull white-glowing prana through all your pores and into your body. Maintain this concentration during the holding of your breath and the exhaling. Since this ability consists of magnetic energy, the following idea may prove helpful. Imagine that you are swimming in the water, and with every breath sucking in the water's magnetic powers.

Traveling with Spiritual Entities

Spiritual Body Travels

A mental journey is a transfer of consciousness from one place to another. In this way, you can visit any place on earth, and also the various spheres of the planets, elementary regions, and other dimensions. The spiritual body is free of time and space. The mental journey is a preliminary stage to travels with the energy body—the astral journey—and its execution is not connected with any great dangers.

You can do this exercise sitting or reclining. The danger of falling asleep always exists when you're lying down, and it needs to be avoided, in any case. Begin with alpha breathing (page 203) and complete relaxation. Bodily feelings need to be forgotten, while your spirit remains wide awake. Then, willfully draw your consciousness out of your body. This happens by mentally thinking yourself out of your body so you can view yourself as an onlooker. Give special attention to details such as facial expression and the position of your hands. When tiredness sets in, end the exercise. After reentering your body, check the details.

When you have had a little experience with this exercise—after several repetitions—you can begin walking around in the room and the house as a spirit entity. Here too, you need to take notice of certain details, whose correctness you can check after the exercise is over. If the perceptions agree, you can be sure that you have actually taken a mental journey.

The next step is to enlarge the field of activity and visit places farther off. In order to test the accuracy of your perceptions once more, it is a good idea to visit a store that you have never been in before and look around in it. On the following day, visit the store in your body and compare the results. If you pass this test, you can begin visiting faraway countries and other worlds. Then you can be sure that real happenings have taken place. In this manner, you can even visit the realm of dreams and influence the occurrences there.

The symbol to the right will help you get into the altered state that is needed to do this mental travel. With it, you can send your spiritual body into other dimensions more quickly and easily. Just concentrate fixedly on the picture until the effects of self-hypnosis set in, effecting the separation of the spiritual body, which will then be

drawn into another dimension through one of the white areas of the symbol.

You'll find other ways of visiting other areas of consciousness with the spiritual body in the chapter "Magic Aids."

Travels with the Energetic Body

Different from mental travel is travel with the energetic or astral body, which is of coarser material than the spiritual body. With it, you can achieve results on the material level. In addition, on an astral journey you are much more likely to experience your own sensations.

Here, too, start in a comfortable sitting or reclining position and let your spiritual body leave your physical body, as described earlier. Then, concentrate on the coarse material body, and with the help of your will, draw your energetic body into your spiritual body. This unification may release unfamiliar, even possibly unpleasant sensations. Suddenly you will miss the feeling of breathing, and with any intuitive reaction of fear or doubt, the energetic body will immediately fall back into the material body. It may take quite some time before you get used to this condition by continually practicing it.

The urge to be drawn back into the material body is especially strong as long as you remain in the vicinity of 33 feet (10m) of it. The energetic link that connects the astral body with the material one is still strong at this distance. To eliminate this effect, you can employ the following procedure: Let the spiritual body wander to a location farther away—to the garden door, for instance—and pull the energetic body into the spiritual body from there. Now, more intense intuitive reactions will be necessary in order to hurl the energetic body back.

It is also possible to leave the material body with your breath. This, however, is a very dangerous procedure. Immediately after the unification of the energetic body with the spiritual body, the breath is pulled along with it. This happens by breathing through the concentrated will. The material body sinks into a deathlike condition without any perceptible breathing, and the supply of air is then continued over the energetic link. You must make absolutely sure that nobody touches your abandoned body, since this would cut the link, resulting in the immediate death of the material body.

When you have permitted the astral body to exit your physical body, you are free to visit all kinds of places. It depends on the level of your development what influence you can exert on the material world. But it is best to avoid visiting other dimensions in the beginning, in the event you have an intolerance toward the vibration of one of the spheres you explore; this could cause bodily, as well as energetic death.

If you are attacked on the astral level, you can immediately withdraw into your physical body. There is no need to fear that the body left behind can be occupied by another entity without your consent.

Mastering the Elements

For a magician who wishes to achieve tangible works by his own power, it is essential to master the elements. The exercises that follow will help you to do it. Their duration should not exceed 15 minutes, at least in the beginning.

The Water Element

Get into a comfortable position and a meditative mood. Then, imagine that the whole universe is an immense ocean and you are swimming in it. By breathing through your pores (see page 206), you draw the water into your body, distinctly feeling its coldness and magnetic strength. Be careful to take the same number of breaths while exhaling the element from your body, as you do when inhaling. After you end the exercise, no strange sensation should be felt.

Through the perfection of this exercise, you will achieve mastery of the water element, and will then be able to bring about a rainfall in the deepest desert.

The Earth Element

Get into a comfortable position and a meditative mood. Then, imagine that the whole cosmos consists of earth. You will experience a distinct feeling of denseness and heaviness. Through the pores of your skin, breathe the earth into your body, while counting the number of breaths. When you feel as heavy as lead, you will have achieved the goal of the exercise. Using the same number of breaths you took while inhaling, you now exhale the element from your body, until your body is back to normal.

You can use the element of earth in many ways—to deal with something that takes shape in the material world. If you can create the element of earth quickly, you can hurl it against an attacker, paralyzing him. Its mastery can even lead to invulnerability.

The Fire Element

Get into a comfortable position and a meditative mood. Then, imagine that the universe is an immense sea of fire. With the aid of your will, you now inhale this element through your pores into your body, counting the breaths. Be careful to perceive distinctly the unfolding of the power of fire. When your body has measurably

Balinese Fire Walker

warmed, you will have achieved the goal of the exercise. You now exhale the element from your body using the same number of breaths that you inhaled, until your body has returned to normal.

If you master the fire element, you will be able to walk in the snow without clothes or cause snow to melt within a vicinity of several miles. You can also light candles that are some distance away.

The Air Element

Get into a comfortable position and a meditative mood. Then, imagine being in an immensely spacious area in which is only air. Suck the air into your body through your pores, counting the number of breaths. Pump yourself up again and again, like a balloon, until you feel as light as air. You have then reached the goal of this exercise. Exhale the element from your body using the same number of breaths that you inhaled, until the sensation of lightness has disappeared.

If you succeed in mastering this element, it will be possible for you to float in the air and transport yourself to a different location without losing any time.

The Ether Element

Get into a comfortable position and a meditative mood. It is important to be completely still. Then, imagine being in the midst of an immensely wide realm of the universe. The aim of this exercise is to attain a feeling of complete removal from the world, in which any sense of time and space is lost. Let the ether stream in and out evenly through your pores. This element is not tangible and cannot be collected in the body the way the other elements can.

If you master the element of ether, it will give you independence from time and space.

Charging with the Power of the Elements

Charging or storing is an extension of the exercises described before. Energy, collected in the prescribed manner, can be conducted through the will into objects, which are magically charged with the energy of the particular element.

Charging for Your Own Purposes

Collect the energy of the desired element in your body, as described. If you have stored enough of it, you can conduct it through your fingers into the object while exhaling, preparing it for its magical use.

Charging for Others

If you want to charge an object for another person, or transfer elemental power into another body for healing purposes, don't conduct the energy of the element through your own body. In such a case, place yourself, as described before, in the realm of the element, but guide its energy through your will directly to its destination. This transfer work may be done several times consecutively.

Charging a Room

If a whole room is to be charged with a certain element, its energy must first be collected in your body and conducted into the room through your hands or the solar plexus. You will know this process has been successful when you feel a noticeable change in the room's atmosphere. With the invocation of elementary spirits (see the chapter "Demons, Elemental Spirits, Sphere Creatures"), it is especially important that the room be charged beforehand with the energy of the appropriate element so that the entity will be able to appear.

After ending the invocation, dissolve the collected energy by guiding it through your will into the cosmos. In that way, you can prevent the room from becoming a wild playground for unwanted elementary spirits.

8.

Working Magic

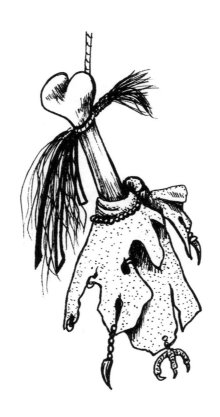

The Basic Steps in an Invocation

- Dressing in magical garments
- Preparing the magical objects, including candles, if necessary
- Drawing the magic circle
- Drawing the magic triangle (if the appearance of a spirit entity is desired)
- Placing the candles and lighting them
- Lighting the incense
- Preparation of sacrificial offerings, if necessary
- Invocation of the cardinal points, beginning with the East (addressing the respective beings, elementary entities, or angles, according to your individual wishes)
- Imaginary sealing of the place from within the circle. The pentagram or the hammer rite (page 264) is suitable protection. (In Haitian Voodoo, however, this step is eliminated. Instead, the magician protects himself by laying down a thick circle of salt.)
- Placing of the magic mirror
- Drawing the vévé of the entity being invoked (if available)
- Loud invocation with the help of a self-chosen or a traditional formula
- Enter a meditative state and wait to establish a contact with the entity, or use a magic mirror. At this point, you can also enter the spiritual or the energetic level.
- The active part can be extended according to your wishes.
- After the end of the invocation, thank the entity for its support and send it off.
- Its vévé is to be destroyed or safely stored.
- Thank and dismiss all other entities involved, as well as the cardinal points, with blessings.
- Dissolve the magic circle. Store the magic objects appropriately.

Runes

All written invocations and formulas can be translated into runes. For one thing, runes have a more powerful emission than common writing; for another, they cannot be read and understood by everybody.

As a short introduction, we are providing a translation of the runes into Latin letters. (This alphabetical correspondence is based on the older alphabet, the Futhark.) More extensive explanations can be found in the appropriate literature, but for the magical work in this book, the following list is sufficient.

A	ᚠ	K	ᚲ	U	ᚢ
B	ᛒ	L	ᛚ	V	ᚡ
C	ᚲ	M	ᛗ	W	ᚡ
D	ᛞ	N	ᚾ	X (ks)	ᚲᛋ
E	ᛖ	O	ᛟ	Y	ᛃ
F	ᚠ	P	ᚦ	Z	ᛉ
G	ᚷ	Q	ᚲ	Ng	◊
H	ᚺ	R	ᚱ	Th	ᚦ OR ᛞ
I	ᛁ	S	ᛋ		
J	ᛃ	T	ᛏ		

The Tattvas

The tattvas are the so-called "souls of the elements." During the day, they alternate in dominance, each tattva ruling for 24 minutes. They strongly influence the general vibration with their individual characteristics.

The success of an action depends on the tattva in which it was begun. If you are in the center of a tattva, you have normally made the right decision in choosing the time. If your senses are trained, you can recognize the predominant tattva by its qualities. With closed eyes, for instance, the tattva color becomes distinct; food has a different taste. These time periods play an important part in the workings of magic and in the invocation of spirits.

Aside from recognizing the tattvas through inner viewing, you can also find out what tattva is presently in effect. To do this, you need to know the time of the local sunrise. The order begins every day with the akasha principle and follows as in the list below. The change from one tattva to another takes place every twenty-four minutes. A cycle, therefore, runs for two hours. Then the next cycle begins again with akasha. The following list will give you all the information you need to do the practical magic work discussed in this book.

Ether-tattva: Akasha; *Color:* Black, dark violet; *Taste:* Bitter; *Supporting activities:* Meditation, teleportation (change of location of a material body through thoughts), reading in Akasha

Air-tattva: Vayu; *Color:* Greenish, light-blue; *Taste:* Sour; *Supporting activities:* All activities that need quick execution; levitation (with the material body); influencing time

Fire-tattva: Tejas; *Color:* Red; *Taste:* Pungent; *Supporting activities:* Achievement, competition, energetic working, mastery of fire

Earth-tattva: Prithvi: *Color:* Yellow; *Taste:* Sweet; *Supporting activities*: Positive, optimistic, invulnerability; everything that is begun here ends well.

Water-tattva: Apas; *Color:* White; *Taste:* Salty, astringent; *Supporting activities:* Everything that is to bring success in the long run; marriages, travel, writings, investments, gambling, speculation.

Altars

Preparations

Before you begin invoking spirits or consecrating an altar, you need to purify the place from all disturbing energies and entities. The traditional procedure is smudging (smoking). You can use incense sticks, if you like, but they do not replace the smudging. To this purpose, place coal and herbs in the smoking vessel—sage, rosemary, thuja, cedar, and tobacco are often used, especially in the Caribbean. Then, the room is smudged in a clockwise direction, beginning near the ground, and the smoke is fanned into the uppermost corners of the room. After this cleansing, the ritual can begin.

Invocation of the Cardinal Points (Africa, Haiti)

The invocation of the cardinal points is always a suitable way to prepare a place of ritual for magic or meditation, and for charging it with effective energies. The procedure is similar to that of other cultures, except that other gods are called. The choice of gods and entities with whom you want to work, and also the duration of the ritual, are left up to you.

Begin with the invocation of the original cosmic powers in the form of a large snake that is biting itself in the tail. This is the wheel of death and rebirth and the guardian of souls. You are free to choose any words you want. It is important that the words mirror your inner feelings.

Then, turn to the East and unite yourself intuitively with the element of air, greeting the entities that inhabit it. Call Obatala, the creative god, the breath of life, and ask for the lightness of the air that it may lend you wings.

Then turn South, to the element of fire. Unite with its power, feel its heat. Beg Oya, the goddess of lightning, and Shango, the fire god, for support. Both give you strength, courage, and vital energy.

Now look in the direction of the West, where the water entities live. Feel the refreshing coolness of the great wave and greet the water nymphs and other water creatures. Call Yemaya and Agwé, the mightiest Loa of the waters, and beg them for health, beauty, and love.

Finally, turn to the North, to the realm of the earth. Greet the big mother, while concentrating on the variety and abundance of nature, and connect yourself to all the beings of this world. Invoke the goddesses Asase-Ya, the voluptuous earth mother, and Aye Mu, the spider mother, who weaves Fate. Ask both for permission to participate in the offerings of this world.

Each invocation is ended with a "Blessed be!" or "So be it!"

Courage Ritual

When fear and doubt plague your thought, a ritual is needed to strengthen your courage. Fears are mighty energies that lead to very undesirable happenings. The patterns that they elicit in a person's aura automatically attract their like—a process that creates a "self-fulfilling prophecy." The patterns and expectations precipitate exactly the events of which you are most afraid. With the aid of the courage ritual from the Voodoo tradition, you can break out of the vicious circle of expectation and confirmation. It is easy to experience no fear—it indicates only a lack of fantasy—but it is an art to master it. Each fear that you overcome helps you to gain power and strength for your own life.

First take a new glass or a crystal chalice that is filled with fresh water from a well or a brook. Then write on a piece of parchment the word "COURAGE" in red ink, tomato juice, red wine, or blackberry juice, and sink it into the water. Observe how the writing slowly dissolves and colors the water red. Concentrate on the colored water and imagine that it is the blood of your enemies.

This exercise is not really about existing enemies, but about fear. Recall the dangerous situations that you have experienced and think about how many other actions would have been possible, if you had been without fear. Then, imagine a phalanx of invisible helpers surrounding you who, with their swords drawn, are ready and willing to fight for your cause.

Finally, begin to sing slowly and in a low voice: "I build my house on my enemies' heads." Repeat this sentence over and over again, louder and louder, stronger and stronger. Demand victory for yourself. When you feel deep in yourself and your own power, the ritual can be ended. Then lift your glass and toast your courage, emptying it in one draught, if possible.

After this ritual, you will feel your strength and be able to make the right decision in difficult situations.

The Home Altar

Here is a description of the basic structure of an altar. You can adorn it according to your needs. You could, for instance, decorate it with objects from nature that have a special meaning for you, or if it is dedicated to a certain god entity, you can embellish it with the corresponding symbols.

The altar is covered by a white cloth on whose corners four stones or crystals are placed. They should be oriented as precisely as possible toward the cardinal points. This will keep the altar fenced off from disturbing foreign influences. Place a chalice or crystal bowl in the center of the cloth, filled with water or clear liquid—in the Voodoo cult, clear, high-proof alcohol is considered to house the spirit, and is used in many rituals. The surface of the liquid must always be free of impurities and you need to renew it as necessary.

Place a white candle in a candleholder in front of the chalice, and some family photos behind it, since family members always have a great influence on you, consciously or unconsciously. In this way, they can be included in the magic work, in which they either support you or cross you. Instead of photos, you could use a figurine or a doll to serve as the core of the altar, standing for the god entity with whom the majority of the work is done. For women, it can be a mother goddess or a witch goddess; for men a god that embodies manly strength and virtues, or one who promotes magic.

Bringing Home a Soul Who Has Lost Its Way

Souls of the deceased often find it hard to leave their earthly domicile, especially if death has taken place suddenly—in an accident, for example. The deceased often remain in an intermediate realm and cannot find a way out of this miserable situation. It is common for such ghosts to hang around near their house or the place in which they died, and they sometimes appear as apparitions. The following ritual serves to disengage yourself from the ghost, thereby setting him free and helping him to enter the next level.

For this purpose, you will need a white cloth, one that comes from the deceased's possessions, preferably one he wore on his body or lay upon. Tear out a piece of it that is large enough to cover the altar structure. The fringes of the material tie your energy to that of the deceased. Then take four stones, if possible from the house or garden of the deceased, and place them on the four corners of the cloth. Scatter flowers on the back part of the altar and put a chalice in the middle. The chalice should have in it spirit water—water with a shot of alcohol. Around the chalice place eight small glasses, filled with water. Into the center of the chalice, put a symbol of rebirth—an Egyptian ankh (a Tau cross with a loop at the top), for example; an X-sign; or an isosceles cross that represents the connection between the world of the living (the horizontal bar)—and the world of the dead (vertical bar).

Now place a picture of the deceased in front of the chalice and put a white candle in a candleholder on top of it. Place some food that the deceased favored on the cloth to the left of the chalice; to the right, put some objects that he might perhaps be missing.

Every day, for a period of nine days, place a new white candle on the picture and burn it, saying a short prayer for the deceased each time and sending him off. During this time, you can go daily to his grave, bringing fresh flowers, putting a candle on it, and eating a meal, if this seems necessary.

Outdoor Altar

In keeping with the location, the outdoor altar is decorated with many things found in nature, such as feathers, shells, stones, leaves, and branches, and is fenced off by stones from its surroundings. Its center also consists of a bowl or a chalice with water and some alcohol. Put a candle directly into the ground in front of the chalice. Then bless the place and thank Mother Earth by placing an apple or a similar fruit on the ground within the altar space. Additional decoration depends on the magic that you want to work.

Eliminating Bothersome Ancestor Ghosts

To begin with, make a list of the names of ancestors who in their lifetime were embodiments of true horror for you. Delineate clearly whether these people were really so bad and domineering, or whether you just didn't like them. Write the names of the truly evil cases on a piece of paper that will quickly decay. Then fetch seven different fruits and a black candle and carry all of it to a remote place in the forest. There, place the fruit on a piece of paper and stick the candle into the middle. Don't light the candle, since all connection to the ancestors are to be broken off. Clearly articulate your wish to completely dissolve all connections with the ancestors and ask the wind to take care of them. Then turn around, leave the forest without looking back, and never return to the place of the ritual. When you get back home, it is a good idea to cleanse yourself with a strong salty bath, for salt repels ghosts.

Love Magic

Knot Magic

This magic is carried out during the waxing moon, preferably on a Friday. You need a red or rose-colored candle and a red string or cord. In addition, incense—love-attracting frankincense—is burned. Light the candle, take the red cord and make a knot in it while saying:

In the name of ...(Venus, Aphrodite, or Erzulie), *may* (name of the person) *fall passionately in love with me.*

Make another knot and say:

May the lips of . . . (name of the person) *long for me.*

Now make a third knot and say:

May the heart of . . . (name of the person) *be aroused by me.*

Continue in this way. Choose whatever words you want. It is recommended for love magic that you tie seven knots in this manner. Each of the knots must be well tied. Put the string under your pillow. Throw the candle into running water.

The same procedure is also used with a black cord for harmful magic. This is done during the waning moon with an invocation of the appropriate gods. Only one knot is tied in this practice.

Healing Magic

13 Eggs

This healing magic comes from the Hungarian witchcraft tradition and is carried out during the full moon. It is used when all other means fail. You need 13 eggs for this process.

The sick person is placed on the ground, if possible, in the light of a full moon so as to increase the magnetic powers. Then use one egg to stroke, section by section, the whole body of the sick person. No area of the skin can be omitted. It works best, therefore, if the sick person is almost, or totally, naked. After you stroke the backside of the sick person, put the egg into another container and repeat the same procedure with the next egg.

The ritual is finished after all thirteen eggs have been used in this manner. Since the eggs have absorbed the illness, you need to throw them into running water, or break them and bury them in the ground.

You can increase the effectiveness of the ritual with the help of the appropriate god entities, such as Diana, Aradia, or the Haitian god Loco, or by including their vévés.

The Sending of Curses

Curses can be sent in many ways. Their effects on the collective unconscious will only become reality if the victim possesses sufficient evil or envy of his own, since the magic principle rests on resonance. Aside from the forms described here, curses can also be sent with the help of Voodoo dolls and wangas (see page 243).

This example illustrates how curses work: The curse picture at the right was created by a poacher in Great Britain. The lord of the manor and his two helpers had banned him from his home. To avenge himself, he formed three of these images and fastened them to the house. After he had regularly cursed them, the lord and his helpers died.

Abandonment Curse

If a witch is abandoned by her lover and betrayed in a particularly despicable way, she probably plans revenge. If the man then enters another relationship or even a marriage out of lowly motives, or because he is seeking advantages through the new relationship, the witch may put the following curse on the couple.

She would go at midnight, during a waning moon, to a cemetery and pluck flowers from three different graves. She would then add a few of her own hairs and tie everything into a bouquet. She would then place it, in the moonlight, on the grave and might say:

Venus, goddess of love, who considers faithfulness and truthfulness the highest virtues, come and hear me. Let...(his name) and... (the name of the other) separate in hate and ire. May they be separated like the sun from the earth, like day and night and never meet. Torture the cause of my pains. May...(his name) and...(the name of the other) never meet. O Venus, make my revenge your revenge.

The formula can of course be changed according to her desire. After the witch has repeated this three or seven times, she removes the bouquet from the grave and places it in front of the unfaithful lover's door.

With an abandonment curse she should make sure that the couple is not truly in love; otherwise, the curse could backfire. If she were to destroy a true love relationship, her own will be destroyed as well.

Curse with Limited Effect

A black candle and a sheet of parchment paper are needed for this curse. The candle is rubbed with a strong oil (camphor, for instance, or cinnamon rind) and then lit. The magician imagines the victim being in the flame. When the face is distinctly visible in front of his spiritual eye, he begins the invocation.

It is up to the practitioner to which god he gives the order. Appropriate for this magic are: Hecate (from Europe); Kali (from India); Gédé Niho and Baron Samedi (both from Haiti). The execution of the curse is delegated to only one of the gods.

The incantation can be similar to the following:

...(God), *I curse*...(name). *May*...(name) *wind himself in pain with stomach cramps for seven days from today on*...(god) *tie up his throat. Let*...(name) *find no rest out of fear*....(God), *throw* ...(name) *into darkness and pursue him with misfortune. This is my desire. So be it!*

Each sentence is immediately written on the parchment after it has been spoken. It is advantageous to use a secret code or runes. Spirit entities prefer uninitiated people who cannot easily decipher runes and other secret writing. Put the prepared note near the victim, preferably under his bed, in his pocket, or under the doormat.

Warning:
If the cursed one does not deserve this treatment, this curse could backfire onto the person who used it.

Wangas

Wangas are objects that have been magically charged by a bokor (black magic practitioner). Depending on the power of the magician, this may have been done during a ceremony or only by incantation or touching. If the intention is to be kept secret, the bokor usually selects a harmless looking object, such as a drinking glass or a stick. An inconspicuous carrier substance is often used: powder and dust, for instance, are favored for harmful magic because they are inconspicuous. Nails or chips are also common, because they are easy to smuggle into the victim's pockets. Illness or even death may be the consequence, if the victim injures himself on them. Wangas are only dangerous for the intended victim; other people, who come into contact with them, remain untouched.

A very common practice with wangas is to instill the fear of a hexed object in the victim. The magician may arrange things in an unusual way and place them so that they catch the victim's eye, inciting conscious and unconscious fears. This can go so far that wangas, made from the cadavers of ritually killed animals and their blood, are placed in front of—or inside—the target person's house. These, and other wangas made in a disturbing manner, serve as a warning to the targeted person to change his behavior or even leave the area. Of course, in such a case, the target person has the advantage of knowing that a sorcerer is going to attack and can take timely countermeasures. Normally, however, wangas are completely inconspicuous, as described before, and remain undetected.

Footprints

As with most magic practices, the following procedure from the European witchcraft tradition can be used for the good of a person or to harm him.

All matter that a living person touches absorbs a part of his energetic emission. It is also this emission that dogs perceive when they follow a scent. In this case, the witch secures footprints of the targeted person and stores them. With footprints, not only is the person's emission available: there is the additional powerful energy of forward movement, the pursuit of a certain intention or goal.

This magician can employ this energy to steer the fate of a person in the direction he chooses. Best suited are prints in fine sand, fine gravel, or moist ground in which the traces are fully visible and well preserved. The magician puts the trace of the footprint on a board or in a pan. He turns the print so that the trace is aimed at a chosen target. It can be another person, a building, a location, or a job. In addition, with the help of dolls, twigs, stones, and other symbolic objects, a situation can be created that is specially intended for the target person. Important for success, here too, is the power of imagination and the intensity of the feeling with which the magic is carried out.

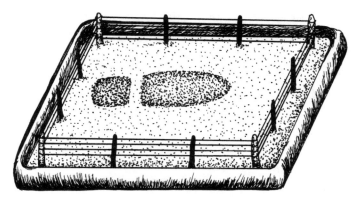

In earlier times such footprints were used to make a traveler stray from his way or to lead him into impassable fields. In another black-magic technique, nails were stuck into the footprints to cause pain or hinder the person from going on to his destination.

The Hairy Hand

This harmful magic has been practiced mostly by witches in the Southwest of England. It is used to bring about hardening of the arteries in the victim. Shapes in the form of a hand are cut from the skin of a cow or a horse. Red woolen threads are then pulled through them with a needle to represent veins. The red thread binds the illness to the victim, and each stitch aggravates the suffering.

Knitting and Weaving Magic

In Europe, especially during the Middle Ages when weaving and knitting were everyday activities, this kind of magic was frequently used. Expressions like "the weaving of fate" or "to spin the thread of life" come from these times. The magic could pertain to someone else or to the witch herself.

Black virgin wool and glass needles were used for the knitting magic. The color black was chosen because it better absorbed the energy. The same incantation was repeated continuously while knitting, until the yarn was used up. The needles were then removed from the knitted piece and it was burned. But the witch had let the magic loose and, by doing that, it gained the strength and vitality of fire.

With weaving magic, the procedure was similar. The finished fabric, however, was not usually burned but made into a piece of clothing for the target person. The recipient could either be protected or harmed by the magic. Certain abilities could also be conferred in this manner.

The Mandrake

The mandrake root has been valued in Europe from time immemorial as a powerful aid. Its spirit is supposedly able to kill a person. In order to unfold its power, the harvesting of the root is tied to a number of rituals and bound to certain times. It should be dug out only in a night of the full moon between Easter and Christ's Ascension, while the harvester must protect himself with amulets against its deadly curse. To be absolutely safe, it was common practice to let a dog dig up the root.

It was already highly valued in Egypt and Greek antiquity for its effects—stimulating the sex drive and bringing about hallucinations. It was assigned to the satyrs, those lusty companions of the old creator god Dionysus. It was also well known in Asia, and in the European witchcraft tradition it was a large part of the so-called flight drink, reputed to give the ability to fly. These mixtures consisted, at least in part, of highly toxic ingredients whose use was not without risks. The mandrake root itself contains some very poisonous substances that can cause dementia and lead to a coma if swallowed in large doses. Aside from the imagined flying, the root gave rise to other hallucinations in people, similar to an LSD trip, and started off many an astral journey (a journey of the energetic body freed from the material body).

Another ritual that comes from the Druids utilizes the powerful spirit of the mandrake to secure the support of forest spirits. Much experience with spirit entities and adventurer blood, however, is a precondition for it. The ritual is called "the wild hunt" and is customarily carried out in during the full moon in October, but can be started in other months on the sixth night after the new moon or on any other night of the full moon.

The Wild Hunt

As a preparation for the "wild hunt," the hunting territory had to be carefully selected and fenced. The ritual place had to be in the forest, and the length of the road to the edge of the territory was approximately half a mile to a mile (1 to 1-1/2km). The Druid had to think about which road he would take to leave the territory and what hindrances he would have to overcome, such as brooks, walls, or inclines. Three hours were traditionally allotted for walking on the road. During this time, the elementary spirits that dwelt in the hunting territory would do everything to hinder the Druid from attaining his goal. If he was nevertheless successful in covering the distance in the time allotted, the spirit entities of the territory would give him support for the rest of his life.

When all the preparations were made, the Druid assured himself that the elementary beings consented to his undertaking. He then determined a date for the hunt. Three nights before that date, he went to the place of ritual in the forest and placed there sacrificial offerings of fruit and bread, while proclaiming in a loud voice his plans and the details of the challenge. He announced the day and the time, described the borders of the territory, and stated the hours he would need to traverse it. It was customary to begin the ritual three hours before sunrise and to end it at daybreak. The Druid could assume that the forest spirits consented to these terms if his offerings were eaten or removed.

When the night of the hunt arrived, the Druid dressed in black, a protective color, and took along a mandrake and a flint. He went to the place of ritual, where he kindled a small fire using wood from the area around the ritual place, and being careful not start a forest fire. He consecrated the fire to the master of the other world and king of the hunt, Gwynn ap Nudd, while loudly speaking the following incantation:

Open glade in the dark forest,
Pine branch in the warrior's hand,
Smoke of mandrake
Sends out the black guardian.
Listen to the fluttering of midnight-wings,
The running of the forestland bear.
Listen to the clatter of courageous souls
In the name of the master of the hunt,
Listen to the breath of the God, wild and dreadful
Listen to the tracks of the terrible hounds.
Listen, how Gwynn ap Nuud
Enters the open clearing in the dark forest.

He then waited until the fire burned out, threw the mandrake root into the remaining embers, and immediately started leaving the territory, for the spirits would soon start to pursue him.

A Druid was not allowed to underestimate the power of the "black guardian." He had to be aware that many hindrances would be in his way to tax his physical and spiritual powers to the limit. Forest spirits were not above putting diversions in the Druid's path to confuse his brain. At daybreak, the spirit of the mandrake lost its power and dissolved.

Should the Druid be forced to the point of having to give up, he only needed to turn around and return to the place of the ritual. The attacks of the forest spirits would then cease immediately. If he did not pass the challenge, he had to pay a sacrificial compensation to the master of the territory, which might have consisted of valuable honey and rare herbs.

*Siberian Tungus-Shaman, turning into his animal shape
(after an 18th-century engraving)*

Transformations into Animals

It is said that some shamans of various cultures can transform themselves into animals. There are many reports confirming this. The best-known form is the werewolf (see the chapter "Demons, Elemental Spirits, Sphere Creatures").

Yet it is known that some sorcerers and witches can change into all possible animal forms. Especially favored are strong animals like bears, hyenas, panthers, lions, crocodiles, or magical animals such as serpents, bats, cats, ravens, and toads. Transformations into insects sometimes occur too—poisonous ones are preferred!

Most shamans master the transformation into an animal form only on the energetic level. That means a kind of blending takes place in their human form. The watchful and clear-sighted observer can then distinctly perceive the animalistic features.

Another form of transformation occurs through the emission of the energetic body. This can be so strongly intensified by a practiced magician, who has worked up in himself the animal characteristics, that his transformation can be perceived even by the uninitiated. He may also be able to physically interfere in the natural processes of the material world.

The least common form of this kind of magic is the transformation of the physical body. Transformations into animals are often the result of a pact that was made with the animal species. This is advantageous to the animal, since it advances its development. The magician promises to protect the animal in every respect. If he does not observe the agreement, he may physically and spiritually suffer serious damage.

Another procedure is the concentrated immersion in another form of life, with senses on all three levels—spiritual, energetic, and material.

Candle Rituals

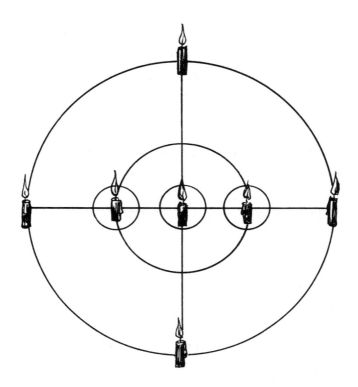

Basic Structure

In order to draw the circle for this candle ritual, the magician uses a powder made from a basic substance and a sweet supplement. Mixtures of millet and lavender, rice and cloves, or wheat and rosebuds are suitable. With this powder, he lays out a large circle on the ground and two lines that cross in the center.

The color of the candles depends on the magic that is to be carried out. One of the candles represents the person for whom the magic is being worked. It is placed on the intersection of the lines in the middle of the circle. Then candles are put to the left and right of it. They represent the energies that are to be attracted. Four more candles in a neutral white color are placed on the four intersecting lines within the circle. They represent the four cardinal points.

If there are no contradictory magical requirements, always let all the candles burn out together. This can take quite a long time, so the ritual can be done over the course of several days.

Making Candle Oil

For many magic works, you can use natural ethereal oils that are available in stores. Oils that cannot be obtained or are too expensive can be homemade. These oils have the advantage of being already charged with the energy of the magic worker.

Use a neutral oil as a base, such as thistle oil, olive oil, sweet almond oil, or sesame oil. Then, select herbs that are appropriate to the magic. Crush them in a mortar until you can clearly perceive their scent. Then mix the crushed herbs with the oil—the quantities to be used depend on the magical requirements—put the mixture in a tightly closed container, and place in a cool location. Let the mixture ferment for at least three days, or even better, for two weeks. The oil is then ready for use.

The Colors

White—*Supports:* Peace, purification, healing, blessings, concentration, clarity, begging for others; *Oils that increase the effect:* Mustard, anis, thistle

Yellow—*Supports:* Attraction, fantasy, invocation, fairies and elves; *Oils that increase the effect:* Yarrow, bergamot, patchouli, cinnamon

Gold—*Supports:* Wealth (also through gambling), solar power; *Oils that increase the effect:* Bergamot, bay leaves, thyme, marigold, seeds of pomegranate

Red—*Supports:* Love, passion, strength, courage, prosperity, vitality;

Oils that increase the effect: Musk, rose, red carnation, red pepperoni, hyssop

Rose—*Supports:* Love, gladness, honor, bitter vibrations; *Oils that increase the effect:* Ylang-ylang, rose, raffia, myrtle

Blue—*Supports:* Success, friendship, protection, peace, happiness, good fortune: *Oils that increase the effect:* Magnolia leaves, valerian, poppy seeds, rosemary

Green—*Supports:* Health, prosperity, abundance; *Oils that increase the effect:* Bergamot, cinnamon, myrrh, nutmeg, coltsfoot, chamomile

Orange—*Supports:* Luck, concentration; *Oils that increase the effect:* Raffia, bay leaves, rosemary, sandalwood

Brown—*Supports:* Influence, stability; *Oils that increase the effect:* Grass, geranium

Purple—*Supports:* Power, concentration, work; *Oils that increase the effect:* Lavender, cinnamon, labdanum

Silver—*Supports:* Seriousness, meditation, moon powers; *Oils that increase the effect:* Lady's mantle, anis, lavender, watermelon seeds, basil

Black—*Supports:* Throwing back, letting go, banning; *Oils that increase the effect:* Garlic, cinnamon bark, rose, camphor, rosemary, St. John's wort, bats' blood (the plant)

The Forms

Small, glazed, wide—*Symbol for:* Votive candle (consecrated gift); *Colors:* all; *Use:* As altar candle

Cylindrical, to be lit on both ends—*Symbol for:* Double-sidedness; *Colors:* black (outside); red (inside); *Use:* To repel magic, for protection/waning moon

Thick, cylindrical—*Symbol for:* Devotion; *Colors:* All; *Use:* For personal magic, praise, and curses

Thick, glazed, cylindrical—*Symbol for:* Seven-day candle; *Use:* According to magic intended, for personal magic / Let candle burn on seven consecutive days for 24 hours.

Seven knots, one over the other—*Symbol for:* Wish; *Colors:* All; *Use:* Wish fulfillment / during waxing moon burn one knot every day.

Figures, general—*Symbol for:* Persons; *Colors:* Gray; *Use:* Purification from illnesses, deliverance from unhappiness and misfortune / waning moon

Woman/man—*Symbol for:* female/male person; *Colors:* Red, white, black, green; *Use:* Red for love magic / waxing moon / musk oil; white as persons' candle; green for prosperity / waxing moon / health; black against attacks and misfortune / waning moon / Let candle burn daily, seven days, for 15-30 minutes.

Black cat—*Symbol for:* Protection; *Color:* Black; *Use:* To put an end to slander, defamation of character / waning moon

Serpent—*Symbol for:* Power, defense, wisdom, spiritual helpers; *Colors:* Red, black, white, outside black / inside red; *Use:* White for wisdom and spiritual helpers; red for elimination of difficulties between lovers; black for defense against enemies; to throw back or repel magic / waning moon, black-red for revenge.

Skull—*Symbol for:* Spiritual realm; *Colors:* black, white, purple / red; *Use:* black against attacks on the spirit, for dissolving a spell; white for healing of the spirit, for learning; purple / red for influencing others spiritually or emotionally, for healing psychic problems, for instance.

Yoni (Vulva)—*Symbol for:* Female sexual organs; *Colors:* All / red, green; *Use:* All for rebirth and freedom; red for love magic; green for health and growth.

Long, slender candles, solidly colored, are used customarily as ritual candles, as well as for individuals. Solidly colored candles have a better color vibration and burn cleaner. The candles should not be scented. For oiling, it is best to use ethereal oils, which can be homemade according to your needs (see page 253).

The Proper Use of Ritual Candles

Oil the candles and charge them with the energy of the magic worker. Put votive candles and seven-day candles (candles in a glass) into a glass of water before they are placed on the altar. The water has magnetic qualities and connects the magic with the ever-present energy field that followers of Voodoo call "DA." This DA can be compared to the magnetic flux of water in the European magic tradition.

You need the following supplies for the candle ritual given here in addition to the person's candle: a small glass—an 8.75 oz (250g) yogurt glass; earth from the garden (can be from a flower pot);

magnetized sand (from the beach, if possible), a few wood shavings; celery seeds; some water sweetened with honey; salt; four coins; the carefully written and folded (see page 258) wish list of the person for whom the magic is being carried out; and a somewhat larger bowl of glass or metal.

Wash the small glass with salt water and then fill it halfway with earth. Bury the wish list deep in the earth, along with the wood shavings. Sprinkle some celery seeds on top and lightly cover with earth. Insert the four coins into the earth so that the head sides point toward the center of the glass (they should still stick out of the earth somewhat). Then, sprinkle the sand over the coins and heap more of it up in the middle of the glass.

Now hold the person's candle tightly with both hands, clearly state the purpose of this magic, and push the candle deep into the sand and earth. Fill the remaining space in the glass with more earth. Moisten the earth with some honey-water and put the glass into the bigger bowl. Fill the bowl with water and take everything to the place of ritual. You can now be certain that the magic is well grounded; the seed is sown.

At the place of the ritual, utter the wish list three times loudly, while you are lighting the candles. Three is the number of the god Legba and of the threefold god entity. When the ritual is finished, it is not necessary to give it any further attention. Dispose of the leftover supplies and the glasses, and go back to your daily tasks.

Wish List

Parchment or wood-fiber paper is used for the wish list, on which the magic worker writes his wishes and magic formulas. For writing instruments you can use fountain pens, quills, or bird feathers that have been given a point. Whichever you choose, use it only for this purpose. Write with ink or india ink in red or black. Pigeon-blood ink and dragon-blood ink are also well suited for the realization of wishes and for repelling negative powers.

Always write the name of the person for whom the magic is being carried out, and the names of his ancestors and their familial connection to him (aunt, great grandfather, stepbrother, son-in-law, etc.). Next, note the date on which you have begun the magic.

Now put the wish in very clear words, formulating it as a request. The wish can be for you yourself or for another person who must then be listed in this place by his full name. The more succinct and direct the words, the better! If you wish for wealth, write down the exact amount. It's a good idea to announce that you are willing to accept an alternative—by doing this, you indicate that you recognize the might and wisdom of the spirit entity. Close with thanks, knowing that your wish is already being realized. Sign the wish list with your full name, or have it signed by the person whose wish list it is.

Prosperity (Haiti)

This magic works best during the waxing moon. Place four white candles on the four cardinal points of the circle. The person's candle may be the same color as his the aura or his favorite color. The candle to the left is golden, for riches, the one to the right of it is green, for nature's abundance.

Health (Haiti)

This magic works best during the waxing moon. Place four white candles on the four cardinal points of the circle. Then, put a white candle in the middle of the circle, and to the right and left of it a green one, so you have seven candles altogether. Light the four candles in the big circle first, then the three in the middle. The outer candles will be completely burned on the first day, so that they will generate the necessary energy field. Burn the inner ones every day for five to fifteen minutes, while you look into the flames and concentrate on the desired result. Each day, move the two green candles closer to the center candle, so that at the end all three are close together.

Mental Abilities (Haiti)

This magic works best during the waxing moon. Place four white candles on the four cardinal points of the circle. The candle in the middle of the circle represents the person for whom the magic is being performed; it should be of a deep rose or neutral white color. To the left, place an orange candle, to the right, a purple one, and continue as before.

Getting Out of a Dead End Situation

This magic helps you to find a way out of a hopeless situation, especially when you have inadvertently hexed yourself.

Place four white candles on the four cardinal points of the circle. In this case, a black banishing candle or one that you can light at both ends is used as the person's candle in the center of the circle. Place a blue candle to the left of it; a white one to the right, and continue as before.

New Love (Haiti)

This magic is most effective on a Friday before the full moon. Place four white candles on the four cardinal points of the circle. The center candle can be either the favorite color of the one for whom the magic is being carried out, or the color of the person's aura. Place a yellow candle to the left (attraction), a red one to the right (passion), and continue as before.

Friendly Atmosphere (Haiti)

Place four white candles are placed on the four cardinal points of the circle. The center candle can be either the favorite color of the one for whom the magic is being carried out, or the color brown, which represents stability. To the left of the person's candle, place a blue candle, to the right a white one, and continue as before.

9.
Protection Rituals

A ttacks from spirits take place constantly in varying strength and in various ways. We need to distinguish, however, between actions carried out deliberately and the involuntary emission of negative energies. Both can be harmful to body and soul. Our sensitivity to disturbing energies depends on our general condition and psychological stability. In general, you could say that negative powers always attack our weak points.

The best protection therefore is increased attention to ourselves and to our own behavior. Even the most dangerous demons a bokor can send out will attack only if they find people with sufficient negative energies of their own—in the form of hate, envy, fear, etc.—since "like attracts like" on the spiritual level.

If it becomes evident after a thorough test that you have been the victim of a magic attack, the first thing to do is to critically check yourself out, asking the following questions: To whom did I willingly or unwillingly cause harm? Is anything questionable about my sense of justice? What behavior of mine, or what attitude, could have attracted the negative energy? Where do my dependencies, my weaknesses, my cravings lie? It may be helpful to make a list of your positive and negative character traits—not to show to anyone, but just to examine and keep in a safe place. It is very important to be completely honest with yourself in making this list!

Protective Symbols

The Freya-Torch

The Freya-torch is a universal protective symbol of the Norse love and fertility goddess Freya. It repels negative energies of all kinds and attracts positive ones. There are many ways to use it in everyday life: mailboxes and telephones, for instance, can be quite effectively sealed against disturbances. It can protect a room from the reach of negative powers, if you attach a picture of it to the wall. But you don't have to have a picture. It will work if all you do is hang a symbol of it in the room in your imagination. In this way, you can have your bedroom protected from spiritual attacks during the night.

Thor's Hammer

Thor is the Norse god of thunder, protector of the earth and humans. His hammer effectively protects the magic area from disturbances of all kinds. The hammer ritual is used to do energetic screening at magical rituals and invocations, sometimes taking the place of the pentagram. The hammer rite that follows is suitable for those who don't like to make a great display.

The Hammer Rite

Turn to face North and, with your right hand, draw the sign of the hammer in the air in front of yourself. Make the movement in the direction of the arrow, while you recite the following formula:

"Hammer of the North, guard this holy place and protect it!"
Then turn to the East and say:

"Hammer of the East, guard this holy place and protect it!"
Now, do the same to the South:

"Hammer of the South, guard this holy place and protect it!"
And now to the West:

"Hammer of the West, guard this holy place and protect it!"
Then draw the hammer on the ground:

"Hammer below me, guard this holy place and protect it!"
Finally, draw it in the air above your head:

"Hammer over me, guard this holy place and protect it!"

Warding Off the Evil Eye

This kind of spiritual attack is not always done consciously. It may have its roots in feelings of envy or hate. It may start to work against you when a strange person simply gives you a spiteful look. The energies are conducted through the eyes.

If you have become victim to the evil eye, you might experience the following symptoms: A strong reduction in energy that can lead to dizziness and, in extreme cases, unconsciousness; nausea that is often followed by vomiting. If you are sure that the cause is not an illness or food poisoning, the evil eye might be playing a role, especially, if you had previously had eye contact with the sender.

If you are constantly in the environment of such people—in the workplace, for instance—it's a good idea to wear an appropriate amulet for protection. The best protection would be a large turquoise, worn around the neck. It is important to cleanse the stone regularly. In the Orient, a blue glass eye on a chain around the neck is used to deflect the evil eye. Small children, and especially babies, may absorb too many unfiltered energies, and they too can be protected in this manner. Of course, it is always possible to counterattack and tell the offender to her face that you feel she is harboring envious thoughts against you. Although this kind of confrontation can become very unpleasant—and attract unwanted attention—the spell will thereby be broken.

Protection from
Negative Energies and Low Entities

Special precautions for self-protection are called for especially during a time of physical weakness—after a separation, for example, or during periods of mourning. As already mentioned, like energies attract each other. Your depression, like a magnet, attracts entities from the intermediate realm who have the same feelings (deceased persons, for instance) or others who are made up of this energy (shadows or phantoms) and feed on them. Such beings are eager to keep you in your depressed state of mind.

If you are in this situation, your body must be ritually cleansed. The first step is usually a cleansing bath. This is best taken in the evening during the waning moon, in natural water—a lake, river, or brook. Salty sea water is also good. You can take a trusted person along for support. The bath should be taken completely naked. While you are in the water, ask the water spirits to remove any negative or strange energies. You could also invoke the water as an element, while imagining that its magnetic powers are drawing all disturbing influences out of your body. If you feel that your condition has changed, leave the water and get dressed in fresh, clean clothes.

If it is not possible to take a bath outdoors, you can also do the cleansing in the bathtub. While bathing, burn cleansing frankincense. You may want to take the following special kinds of baths:

■ White herbal cleansing bath with 2 to 4-1/4 quarts (2-4 liters) of milk and a handful of anis (plant or seeds). Wash yourself with salt. This bath cleanses the body and the aura.

■ White or blue foam bath with a handful of dried or fresh rosemary. (Caution: not suitable for women who are just undergoing their menses.) Wash yourself with soap in the shape of a shell, or with salt.

■ Oak bath for the strengthening and cleansing of the spirit. Add one or two handfuls of clean oak leaves to the bath water. During the bath, establish a mental connection to the strengthening energies of the oak trees.

All used herbs and soaps must immediately be removed from the house and thrown away after bathing, since they have absorbed negative energies. After the cleansing, dress in fresh clothes.

When the bathing is finished, do an extensive smudging with cleansing or banishing herbs, such as sage, sweet grass, St. John's wort or mistletoe. Thoroughly cleanse the whole house from the basement to the attic, moving counterclockwise and distributing the smoke as you go, especially into all corners of the rooms. A good airing should be done later.

To protect yourself from renewed attacks during the following period, it helps to wear silk or black clothes, since spirit energies cannot penetrate these materials. That's why black is considered a color of mourning in most cultures—it protects the mourner from spirit attacks in a time of psychic weakness.

In addition, the following exercise will stimulate your body's own energies and lift your mood:

Stand and stretch your arms to the sides. Make your hands into fists with your thumbs propped up. Then, look fixedly at your right thumbnail and turn 33 times clockwise (to the right), around your own axis. Finally, fold your hands in a prayer-like position in front of your chest and concentrate on a fixed point. Keep the point in view until the feeling of dizziness subsides. In this posture, you will be able to formulate your wishes very effectively. Furthermore, this exercise pulls back split-off parts of the soul, thus strengthening your power. Do this exercise three times daily, if possible. In time, you will become aware of a strong rejuvenating effect.

Repelling Magic

If someone is continually tormenting or harassing you or one of your family members, either on the material or the mental level, you can carry out the following ritual during the waxing moon. It comes from the European witchcraft tradition and is very effective. This magic is solely for self-protection. Remember that even if you are the victim in this case, you are wholly responsible for the extent of the damage you do.

Spread a black cloth as a base and place a white candle on it on the right and left sides. Then take a picture of the goddess Hecate or make a drawing of her (the drawing on page 269 shows the goddess; you can use it as a model) and put it in the middle of the black cloth. Now engrave a black candle three times with the name of the target person. Rub it with the juice of a dieffenbachia (a common houseplant also called "dumb cane") and say:

The tongue of…(name) *shall become mute and fail him, when he/she is spreading lies about me and saying untrue things.*

Next, roll the candle in spider webs and say:

May…(name) *be caught in the net of his/her own intrigues and viciousness.*

Then place the candle in the middle of the black cloth, before the picture of Hecate. In addition, write the name of the victim on a piece of parchment paper.

With the greeting of the fire spirits, light the white candles and then the black one. Burn the parchment paper with the name on it, while you say:

Here is…(name) *alone and helpless, emptiness and failure accompany you. May sorrow and desperation consume you. Stop torturing me or Hecate's ire will come over you! O Hecate, avenging mother, assist me in my work and help me. Let justice prevail. Destroy the plans of...(name). So be it by the might of the lady of darkness!*

You can adapt the magic formula to the situation. When the candles have burned down, it is good to burn some cleansing incense. And be sure to wash your hands after working with the juice of the dieffenbachia, which is toxic. Then collect all the left-overs and wrap them in parchment paper. After darkness has set in, burn the package in front of the target person's house or on a road that he surely will use. In most cases, the person targeted will change his attitude or he will be stricken by the curse and lose the power for further attacks.

Protective Magic Formulas

I f you are certain to be surrounded by strange beings that may do damage in some way, you can try out the following formula. It dates back to biblical times and involves calling out a word nine times consecutively in a diminishing pattern. The word, "abracadabra," means "from now on." The verse banishes unwanted spirit entities of all sorts.

Abracadabra
Abracadabr
Abracadab
Abracada
Abracad
Abraca
Abrac
Abra
Abr
Ab
A

You can also successfully use this formula for healing treatments. Write it on a piece of paper and carry it on your body as a protective amulet.

The next formula has been very successful in dispelling obnoxious elementary entities. Almost every house has these occupants. No flower, for example, would bloom without the help of the fairies. But, every now and then, these beings can become bothersome or even dangerous, since they naturally like to play tricks. You may begin to notice the handiwork of the especially spiteful ones when there are constant noises in the house; several electric appliances breaking down one after another within a short time; when accidents in the household become numerous; cables burn out; you can hear noises in the electric circuits; or documents disappear that only much later, or never, reappear.

Before you carry out an involved exorcism, try this saying. You need to call it out loudly three times in a row:

> *Sylph disappear,*
> *Undine wind yourself,*
> *Salamander burn out,*
> *Gnome take care.*

Protection During Sleep

To protect yourself from nightly attacks, you can equip your bed with a magic lightning rod. This is especially useful, if you are involved with the invocation of demonic entities. You need a long copper or metal wire and a magic dagger or a magic sword. Wrap the wire around the dagger and then wrap it once around all the legs of the bed. Fasten the other end of the wire to the dagger, which you put on the ground with the point down. Better yet, ram the dagger a short distance into the floor. Its function is to conduct the negative energies into the ground.

Cleansing of the House

When the mood in the owner's house is low and a depressing atmosphere exists, it's time to thoroughly free the house from negative energies and spirit entities. This is done on the second or third day after the full moon with a broom, preferably made of birch twigs. If you want to work with the Haitian gods, fasten some ribbons to it in Oya's colors (see page 29). Thoroughly sweep the house with this broom. First, create a left-rotating energy whirl (counterclockwise—see page 145) in every room, and then sweep all negative energies out the door. Do one room after the next and until you have finally chased all the spirits out of the house. To banish them, hit the threshold three times with the broom. Finally, you need to smudge the house with cleansing or banishing incense. If the smoke spreads evenly in the room, without forming whirls, the procedure was successful.

In earlier times, witches used so-called "witch balls" to keep negative entities from entering the house. These balls were of blue or green glass and had a diameter of about 7 inches (18cm). They were hung up in the house and were regularly polished. Feng-Shui crystals, which are presently in vogue, have a similar effect. You can also hang long, narrow flags in the corners of the rooms to repel foreign energies. This is especially suitable for bedrooms.

Expelling Ghosts

A ghost usually does its tricks in a convenient location—in a house, a certain room, or in the place where the person died. Such ghosts wander through an intermediate world, unable to find their way into the hereafter. Many of them do not know that they are dead. Most are therefore very dissatisfied and bewildered. By their presence, they transmit their mood to the living that are in their environment. This can cause an increased aggressiveness in the family. Ghosts also carry out physical attacks sometimes, and appear visibly as shadows, fog, or ghostly forms. If you're sure about the presence of a ghost in the house, the following ritual will be helpful:

Begin the expulsion of the ghost either soon after or before the night of the full moon. In the evening, when everything is quiet, sit down in the room that is most affected by the spooky happenings. Light a candle and get into a meditative state. If you know the name of the deceased, you can address him directly; otherwise, keep the address neutral. As an introduction, ask the ghost to acknowledge his presence with a sign. This can be a noise or a current of air, etc. Then continue speaking to the ghost. First, inform him that he is no longer among the living. Many ghosts are not aware of their condition, especially if they died suddenly and unexpectedly. Once you let him know this, you need to convince him that it is extremely important to go into the light, since only in this way can he continue his further development. Make it clear to him that only in that way can he end his suffering and begin a new life. Your success will depend on your powers of persuasion. You can follow with the spiritual eye whether the ghost follows your advice. If you aren't able to do this, the next few days will show whether the atmosphere has changed and the attacks have ended.

Repelling Curses

Magicians use this procedure when a curse has been uttered openly and the sender is therefore clearly known. The practice is quite adventurous, but also effective. The magician has to get nails—from a coffin. To obtain them, he needs to find an older, remote grave and visit it at night with a shovel. First, he has to ask the death demon, Baron Samedi (see page 50) for his consent, while hitting the shovel three times against the gravestone. Then he puts a plate with eggs, potatoes, or some chicken near the grave, and begins his work. He has to dig deep enough so that he can get to the coffin and remove some nails from it. This is not too difficult with an old grave, since the wood has also rotted. While pulling out the nails, he recites the following:

Coffin nails, confidantes of worms and maggots and other creatures of the darkness, carry out my task of destruction when I order you to do so!

After he gets the nails, the magician immediately puts the grave back in order and wipes out all traces that he has been there. He keeps the nails at home in a small, dark box until he is ready to use them. For security, he takes a cleansing bath after his cemetery adventure and burns banishing incense.

To repel the curse, the magician has to use an object from the sender's possessions. A few hairs or scraps of cloth from the offender's garments would be sufficient. He would drive a few of the coffin nails into them, while reciting:

...(Name) shall suffer himself the horrors of the grave, never again shall...(name) see the sunlight. The curse thereby returns to you...(Name) shall leave the world. Hell now has you. Be it so!

If the magician wants to work with a god entity, he inserts the name of the god into the incantation.

If it is too difficult to secure a personal object, he can replace it with a picture of the attacker and drill the coffin nails through that.

Should the sender meanwhile have retracted the curse, the magic can be withdrawn by pulling the nail out of the object. The object in addition must be washed with salt

Expelling Demons

If you are convinced that your home is inhabited by demonic entities, you might proceed as follows:

First, obtain banishing incense. A proven mixture is deadly nightshade (or thorn-apple) and dragon skin. You also need a magically charged sword.

All the people present in the house would need to be cleansed and protected by smudging, including the animals, since the entity could hide in one of them. Then, all rooms need to be smudged, systematically and thoroughly. After this work is done, walk through the whole house, basement and attic included, and strike in every direction with the magic sword. Supply each room with a magic symbol. You could use the pentagram (drawn in the banishing formula), Thor's hammer, or the Freya-torch.

If the cleansing was done properly, you will surely be free of further demonic activity for a while. Nevertheless, it would be a good idea to explore the reason for the demon's presence.

If the entity should invade again, it would be a good idea to proceed according to the instructions in the section "Dealing with Demons."

Exorcism of Demonic Possession

Possession by a strange entity may be revealed by the following signs: The victim reacts in an unfamiliar way. He becomes argumentative for no reason and eventually speaks in a different voice. His choice of words deviates from his usual way of expressing himself and his glance is changed. You may observe impulsive or suddenly sadistic tendencies.

If possession has been proved with certainty, you can begin with the exorcism. As a start, put the possessed on a diet that cannot contain eggs or meat, since demonic entities prefer to feed on them. After some days, give him two or three glasses of sage tea and have him recite a protective mantra. The mantra "Ong namo, guru dev namo," a protective mantra from Kundalini yoga, has been effective. The words are sung in a long drawn out way and combined with his breathing: "Oooong namoooo"—after the first inhale—"guru dev namoooo"—after the next.

It would be wise for you to sing the mantra several times, too, in order to protect yourself. The possessed will probably reject the sage tea or throw it up. Watch his behavior carefully, in any case. If the demon is willing to talk with you through the mouth of the possessed, you can ask what its demands are in return for leaving the body. If the request is acceptable, you can make a contract. The demon often demands a sacrifice consisting of some pounds of flesh or sausage. Sometimes, it demands a poisoned animal that it can possess in place of the person, a poisonous spider, for instance, or a toad. If the demon, however, demands another family member, do not under any circumstances agree to it!

If you reach an agreement, determine a time and place for carrying out the sacrifice. Offerings are usually taken into the forest or buried. The best times are during a full moon, a new moon or the sixth night of the waxing moon. The demon in return must promise to leave his host instantly.

These entities, as a rule, frequently agree to a deal, since they may go empty-handed if an exorcism is performed. It is important to burn banishing incense after the session has ended and eventually clean the entire house. The affected person should also take a cleansing bath.

Throwing Back a Demonic Possession

If a person exhibits the typical symptoms of demonic possession, and it becomes evident that the cause is some kind of magic or spell, an exorcism can be done so that it falls back onto the sender.

While you are preparing for the exorcism, do not let the possessed person eat any meat or eggs. After administering sage tea, ask the entity to reveal itself. This can take place either directly through the mouth of the possessed or through a dream appearance. It helps to get the demon's name. Some of these creatures betray themselves by certain signs in their living quarters. Always search the lodgings for such clues. Also ask for the name of the sender. After these questions have been answered, you can proceed in two ways. In both of them you will need to use a magic wand.

In one procedure, you draw the name and/or the vévé of the entity on the ground next to the possessed, and also the sign of the Petro-Loa and Legba's vévé. Put a circle around all the signs. Place offerings of fresh meat and eggs on the sign of the demon, and administer sage tea or garlic to the possessed. Burn cleansing incense at the same time. Then sit down in front of the circle, point the magic wand to the offerings and urgently implore the demon to leave the body and accept the offerings in its place. If you feel a vibration of the wand or a light vibration of the ground, the demon has entered the offering. When you are sure that the entity is inside the offerings, carry them out and bury them or place them by a tree in the forest. Destroy the vévés and dismiss any entities that participated or were called for help. Finally, burn banishing incense and get all the participants to undergo a ritual cleansing, as described in the beginning of this chapter.

The second procedure is different in that you work together with the demon. First you ask the entity the reason for its mission. If the possessed person is not seriously guilty of any transgression, and the possession has just been caused by the spitefulness of a bokor, chances are good that the demon can be moved to cooperate. First, you need to make clear to the demon that there is no compelling reason for its presence, and then offer a trade. Promise the demon to make an offering at a certain location and day, outside the house (this promise must be kept under all circumstances). Then place a mirror in front of the possessed. Point to the door of the mirror with the magic wand and summon the demon with the following or similar words:

> ...(Name of the demon), *I implore you, to leave the body of* ...(name) *and return to the one who sent you. Punish the torturer with pains*...(name of the demon), *occupy him and never let him find rest. By the power of the dark powers the mirror's door will close behind you. Be it so!*

You will be able to feel the demon's entrance into the door of the mirror by the vibrations of the magic wand and perhaps as a shadow in the mirror.

After the ritual is ended, all participants must take a cleansing bath.

Freeing a Person from an Elementary Being

Possessions of this kind are often more difficult to recognize than demonic ones. The symptoms are often an ongoing weakness in the victim that finally leads to serious illness. The entity can often be perceived and recognized only by clairvoyant persons. If it is a goblin, use the following procedure:

A night of the full moon is suitable for the ritual. In the early morning hours, before sunrise, take the affected person to a brook or pond that contains a lot of mud. The person needs to take a bath in it, while you go to a place a few yards away. There, you offer the earth spirit an apple and draw a magic circle around yourself. Place the offerings for the goblin—glittering costume jewelry and crystals—in a bowl outside the circle. Invoke the elementary entities, asking them for support. Then sit down and wait.

When the affected person has completely covered himself with mud, the goblin will no longer recognize him as a human being but only as an earthly being. In this exact moment, call the goblin and point to the offerings with the magic wand. In most cases, the goblin will rush to the unexpected gifts. He thereby has agreed to leave his host. Unusual noises and vibrations often accompany this action. The formerly possessed person can now leave the mud bath. Dismiss all participants and dissolve the circle. Leave the place of the ritual at sunrise. On the way back, recite a mantra or discuss other things.

Repelling a Curse,
According to Haitian Rites

If you are certain that an illness or weakness is the result of a magic attack, search the house for strange magic objects or notes with symbols or illegible letters. Be sure to look under the bed and in coat and jacket pockets. A transmission might also have been made through a needle. Be sure to look under the doormat, and check to see if someone could have buried something in the garden. If you find a suspicious object, immediately wash it with salt and take it out of the house. Even when nothing of the kind is found and you do not know who the attacker is, the following repelling magic will be effective. Only carry it out on Fridays.

First, prepare incense from mistletoe, St. John's wort, and plantain. Mix it with some drops of olive oil. Engrave the vèvès of Legba, Loco, and Damballah in a white candle. Then light the incense, hold the white candle in the smoke, and recite the following:

Loco, someone has sent me an illness and cursed me. Take this illness from me. Damballah, someone has sent me loneliness. Free me from the loneliness. Legba, someone has sent me a curse and robbed me of my strength. Give me new strength and power. O, mighty Loa, I will reward you with rich gifts. Send the curse back to the one who is tormenting me!

The smoke opens the door to the realm of the Loa, and through it the powers of the gods merge with the candle. Put the leftover ashes from the incense into a lockable container with 5-1/2 quarts (5 liters) of vinegar and a large fresh bulb of garlic. Let the mixture ferment for a week in the closed container. On the following Friday, take a hot bath and pours two thirds of the mixture into the bath water. Then light the white candle.

To retain the effect of the magic mixture, use only the bath water for rinsing your hair. When you have finished washing, let the candle burn about one third of the way down. Extinguish the flame, wrap the candle in silver foil or in silk, and store in a safe place.

Repeat this ritual bathing on the following two Fridays in the same manner. Then throw the end of the burnt candle into some water. Make an appropriate offering to the participating Loa on the Friday of the following week. A gift of eggs and fruit is gladly accepted.

Protection Against the Curse Of the Deceased's Expedition

This is a practice that Haitians use to free themselves from curses. Like many rituals of Voodoo, it is very involved and cannot be duplicated outside of Haiti.

If a conspicuous little pile of earth is found on your doorsill, it is important to act quickly. Immediately sweep it up and put it into a white linen sack. Dip the sack in rum or another strong alcoholic drink. In this way, the spirits become intoxicated and are unsuccessful when they try to use the earth from the cemetery as an entrance door. Then take the linen sack to a cemetery immediately and bury it in the earth. Make an offering of food, flowers, and water.

If the curse is noticed too late, an experienced magician must be called for help. The appropriate ritual is very cruel. The cursed person is exposed to a shock. Then, the victim assumes a death-like state, which irritates the spirits, causing them to leave the unusable body and instead invade the offerings. Usually, eggs are used for the offering, and they are hurriedly buried after the expelling procedure.

The house is sealed against further attacks with protective magic—generally an object with magically charged herbs that is buried in front of the house.

The death expedition is a particular kind of black magic that is only practiced in Haiti. You would probably never be confronted with such a curse anywhere else.

Bringing Back Zombies

The same is true of the transformation into a zombie (see page 77). To return a zombie's soul to his body, the magician uses the poison of the datura plant (angel's trumpet). He mixes the leaves with animal fat and applies them to the zombie's temples, and the bends of the arms and knees. Some leaves are placed in his mouth. The magician breaks the spell with continuous invocations, calling forth the zombie's soul and commanding it to re-enters its body. When the zombie shows normal reactions again—that is, when life is returned into him—he must immediately be taken to the nearest hospital to extricate the poisons that have been administered (datura is a poisonous plant).

Pulling Out the Soul

A ritual called the "Pulling out of the Soul" is a common method that Voodoo followers use to protect themselves from spiritual attacks. It is a precautionary measure that is particularly valuable to those who practice magic or expect an attack.

The affected person has a hungan (Voodoo magician) carry out the involved procedure. Some hairs from the head, some pubic hairs, and the finger- and toenails of the left side of the body are put into a prepared pitcher. The hungan kills a rooster and, together with the patron, consumes it. The bird's feathers are also put into the pitcher. The magician seals the pitcher and stores it in the altar room. There, it is safe from magic attacks.

The soul is, of course, not really "pulled" during this procedure, but an energetic connection with the hungan's powers and his god entities is established.

Dealing with Demons

I personally am not an enthusiastic follower of involved rituals, but prefer a more direct way of proceeding. This has proved valuable in many cases. Very complicated rituals function something like a cookbook. This is because they have been carried out many times, as you can especially observe in Haitian Voodoo. But the rituals are used because the true connections behind them are not understood.

I would like to underscore once more that a spiritual attack can only be successful if the victim himself has sufficient negative energies. Self-knowledge, therefore, is the best protection of all. But despite that, it can happen that, in a condition of weakness, you can have a demon sent you by a bokor. If this happens, I advise you to establish a direct connection with the being. All that you need is a little courage. These beings are, for the most part, quite open to a direct address and absolutely fond of a trade, since they have nothing to lose.

As a precaution, dress in silk when you are dealing with a demon. Ask it to appear or make itself known by other means. You can ask it to appear in a dream, if a different means of contact is not possible. It then is of major importance to make it clear to the demon that he has been sent unjustifiably, and that no objectionable deed has been committed. After you have presented these facts, ask the entity to reveal on what conditions it will end the attack or the possession.

In most cases, the demon will ask for adequate offerings in the form of meat, eggs, sausage, and other food items. Since demons also go along with modern sensibilities, they will seldom ask for a living animal. (This also depends on the cultural environment and the affected person's ethnic outlook.) When the price for detaching has been determined, the time and place of the delivery must be set. Making this agreement is like making a contract and it must be honored by both sides.

After the retreat of the being, a cleansing bath and a purifying smudging must be undertaken.

In general, demonic beings often agree to a trade, especially if the victim is indeed guiltless. If, however, a being should be stubborn, you can have it banished with the aid of an exorcism. It is not always a good idea to send the demon back to the sender, because, in that case, the sender might become aware and perhaps plan a more dangerous surprise attack.

Index

Index

Index

Index